A

Opinion

Written for the *Young Guardian* 'Input' column, between 1987 and 1988, this collection of twenty-nine articles on topical and controversial matters in the news makes challenging reading.

Often highly critical of the establishment, and written in an ironical and biting style, these pieces present a very personal point of view – one that you may agree or disagree with, but one that is impossible to ignore.

Whether he is protesting about the Obscene Publications Bill, CIA involvement in Nicaragua or the depletion of the ozone layer, Terry Jones reveals a preoccupation with such vital issues as peace, justice, ecology and poverty, and a genuine concern for humanity.

An exciting, witty and thought-provoking collection, brilliantly illustrated by satirical cartoonist Gerald Scarfe.

Terry Jones read English at Oxford University and is probably best known as a member of the Monty Python team. He is also the highly acclaimed author of *The Saga of Erik the Viking*, a modern collection of *Fairy Tales* and his novel for children, *Nicobobinus*. He has also recently published a collection of comic verse.

+ *Plus* ▶

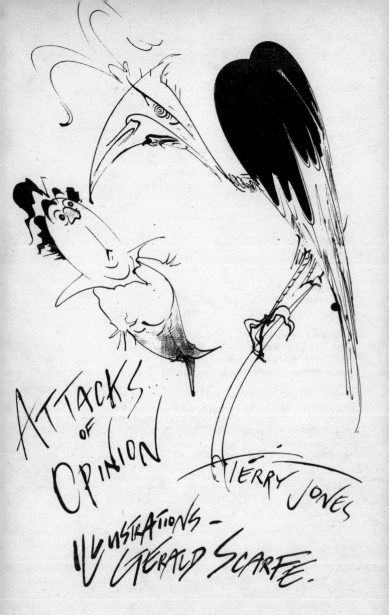

ATTACKS of OPINION

TERRY JONES

ILLUSTRATIONS - GERALD SCARFE.

PENGUIN BOOKS

PENGUIN BOOKS

Published by the Penguin Group
27 Wrights Lane, London W8 5TZ, England
Viking Penguin Inc., 40 West 23rd Street, New York, New York 10010, USA
Penguin Books Australia Ltd, Ringwood, Victoria, Australia
Penguin Books Canada Ltd, 2801 John Street, Markham, Ontario, Canada L3R 1B4
Penguin Books (NZ) Ltd, 182–190 Wairau Road, Auckland 10, New Zealand

Penguin Books Ltd, Registered Offices: Harmondsworth, Middlesex, England

First published 1988

10 9 8 7 6 5 4 3 2 1

Filmset in Linotron Times by
Rowland Phototypesetting Ltd, Bury St Edmunds, Suffolk
Made and printed in Great Britain by
Cox and Wyman Ltd, Reading, Berks

CONTENTS

INTRODUCTION

These short pieces (550–600 words each) were originally written for the *Guardian* newspaper. They appeared every Wednesday as the 'Input' column in the *Young Guardian* between 1987 and 1988.

I was originally invited to contribute to four issues, but somehow I found it was rather difficult to stop once I'd got going, and I would like to thank Tim Madge, the Editor of the *Young Guardian*, for allowing me to vent my spleen every week in his columns.

I would also like to thank him for keeping me to such a short brief. Although I frequently had to cut things out, the pieces almost invariably improved in the shortening. I suspect most things do – including introductions.

Terry Jones
March 1988

AN OBSCENE BILL?

Am I mad or did 183 grown-up men and women gather together last week in our seat of government and actually debate Gerald Howarth's Obscene Publications Bill without collapsing into a heap of helpless laughter? No! Here it is in Saturday's *Guardian* . . . But wait a minute! I must be mad after all, because according to this report, not only did not a single MP collapse with the giggles during the debate but the Bill actually got a second reading! This means that 160 men in long trousers and women over the age of puberty actually voted in *favour* of a Bill that has been framed with all the philosophical insight of Bernard Manning.

The *Guardian* headline on Saturday ran: COMMONS VOTES TO CURB SEX ON TELEVISION, but, reading through Gerald's Bill, that seems to be only a small part of it. The real meat lies in the intention to change the definition of obscenity.

My dictionary defines 'obscene' as 'offensive or outrageous to accepted standards of decency or modesty'. But in an age when such standards are continually shifting and being redefined, it's notoriously hard to pin-down exactly what we are talking about. This is why the 1959 Act tried to restrict prosecution to what might actually be thought to be harmful – although that in itself is a very debatable point.

1

But now Gerald's Bill seeks to move the goal-posts even further back. Forget about whether the material is likely to 'deprave and corrupt'; the new Bill seeks to outlaw anything that 'a reasonable person would regard as grossly offensive'. Now quite apart from the impossibility of deciding whether it is myself or Dr Rhodes Boyson who is a 'reasonable person' (clearly we can't *both* be), what on earth is so wrong about being *offended* by something? Is it really a good idea to start putting people into prison merely because they offend us? Gerald Howarth's Bill is about sex and it offends *me*, so is the Bill itself, by its own definition, obscene?

Commons votes to curb sex on television

By Alan Travis

The attempts to strengthen the obscenity laws and for the first time bring television within their scope won strong backing from the Prime Minister

But why on earth did only twenty-three consenting adults in the House of Commons vote against this Bill? I would have thought that the ending of free speech in this country would have been a matter of at least passing interest to opposition MPs. But then, perhaps I'm not a reasonable person. In fact, perhaps, I'm already well on the way to the cuckoo farm.

The more I think about it, the more I wonder whether Gerald's Bill may not be a blessing to the nation after all. I mean, just think: whether or not you liked *Sebastiane* will no longer be a matter of taste – it will be a matter of law, of prison cells and iron bars. Those who didn't like *The Singing Detective* will no longer have to restrict themselves to grumbling over their brandies or writing to the BBC about the taxpayers' money – they will be given a fair crack at sending Dennis Potter to gaol! How therapeutic for those suffering from gout and heart disease in the Tory shires! Apoplectic of Addlestone and Disgusted of Dorking will no longer have to gnash their teeth in the lonely company of their own prejudices; they will be able to vent their spleen in the courts of law. Who knows how much the crime rate in the home counties may go down as a result?

And what of the artists and writers and directors? Surely they can see the fun of it all? With Gerald's Bill on the statute book their trade will carry an additional thrill. As if the excitement of wondering whether the critics will praise or damn their work weren't enough, there will now be the additional titillation of wondering whether or not they'll get sent to gaol for it. And why not? Isn't that how they ordered things in the Middle Ages? The king didn't find the jester's jokes funny any more? Very good – off with his head!

Oh! Wait a minute! The penny's just dropped! Weren't they also debating capital punishment last week? Of course, unlike Gerald's Bill, it didn't get a second reading, but next time they start talking of bringing back the rope, I'm going to look through the small print just to check they haven't sneaked in an extra clause about 'evil murderers, terrorists and comedians who fail to make a reasonable person laugh'.

Hey ho! Roll on the Middle Ages . . .

8 April 1987

THE COMPENSATIONS OF NUCLEAR POWER

Have you heard what that damn fool William Waldegrave – the so-called 'Green' Minister at the Department of the Environment – has been wittering on about now? Of all idiot ideas, he's suggested that anyone living near a nuclear power station could be paid compensation or helped to move away. Of course, he doesn't say what counts as 'near', but if Chernobyl's anything to go by, a couple of thousand miles is near enough. This means that every man, woman and CND activist on these isles would be eligible for compensation! Either that, or they could be 'helped to move away' – and if they were all 'helped to move away' from these shores, there wouldn't be anyone left to generate electricity for and, therefore, no reason to have nuclear power in the first place!

Children near N-plants 'run increased risk of leukaemia'

By Andrew Veitch,
Medical Correspondent

Children living near five nuclear plants run what is suspected to be a four-fold greater risk of dying of leukaemia, scientists report today.

The plants are: the British

kaemia, scientists reported last week.

There was a serious possibility that nuclear waste was to blame, Sir Richard said yesterday, but there was still no proof.

Sir Richard's team has reana-

the risk of contracting phoid leukaemia with children living away, explained Dr Darby, a team member. were four times as deaths from lymphoid mia in children

Doesn't Waldegrave realize how dangerous such tom-fool ideas are? Doesn't he realize that without nuclear power the entire human race is unquestionably doomed within the next forty or fifty years? The fact that we have existed for several thousand years without nuclear power has nothing to do with the case . . . it only goes to show how lucky we were to invent it so shortly before we realized we were doomed without it. And the fact that nobody ever realized we were doomed without it *before* we had it, only goes to show that you shouldn't trust the experts . . . unless, of course, they are experts employed by the nuclear power industry.

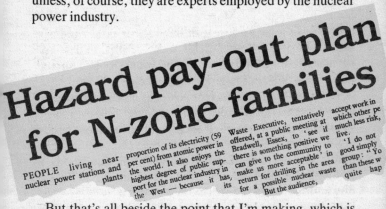

Hazard pay-out plan for N-zone families

PEOPLE living near nuclear power stations and plants proportion of its electricity (59 per cent) from atomic power in the world. It also enjoys the highest degree of public support for the nuclear industry in the West — because it has, its

Waste Executive, tentatively offered, at a public meeting at Bradwell, Essex, to 'see if there is something positive we can give to the community to make us more acceptable' in return for drilling in the area for a possible nuclear waste But the audience,

accept work in which other pe much less risk, live.

'I do not good simply group: "Yo than these w quite hap

But that's all beside the point that I'm making, which is that William Waldegrave's idea of compensating people who live near reactors is not only dangerous but also ridiculous.

My suggestion is that people should be made to *pay* for the privilege of having a nuclear power station at the bottom of their garden. I mean isn't it a privilege to be able to play one's part in the saving of the human race which otherwise will unquestionably die out in forty or fifty and so on and so on?

Besides, nuclear power stations are very attractively designed nowadays – and they *don't* interfere with tele-vision reception (which is more than you can say for trees and mountains). And, in any case, nuclear power stations should *enhance* the value of your property, not detract from it. For a start, they bring jobs and reputation to otherwise undistinguished and remote little villages. It was a nuclear power station that put Three Mile Island on the map (and don't listen to those killjoys who claim it almost took it off it as well). It was a nuclear power station that made Windscale a household name – even (and this is the point) *even when it was changed to Seascale!* Nuclear power has brought fame to individuals too numerous to mention (although Karen Silkwood and Hilda Murrell spring to mind immediately). Moreover it has provided countless others with jobs – not just in the nuclear power industry itself, but also in other fields such as: private-detective agencies, counter-terrorist organizations, public surveillance units, infiltration groups and, of course, MI5.

This country needs nuclear power as much as it needs an armed police force, telephone tapping and ever more stringent surveillance of all enemies of government policy.

Irresponsible lefties like Waldegrave can only do irreparable damage to some of this country's finest traditions, as well as hasten the end of the entire human race in forty or fifty and so on and so forth . . .

Heavens above! Compensate people for living near nuclear power stations, and before long we'd have all the trouble-makers and malcontents in the country demanding

Nuclear plant workers raised safety fear

By Tony Heath

Workers at Trawsfynydd nuclear power station, where a reactor experiment is due to be conducted next month, have complained about declining safety standards, it emerged yesterday.

In another development Mrs Thatcher told a Welsh MP in the Commons that two tests, similar to the one planned for the plant in north Wales, had already been conducted.

Concerns about safety standards at the Trawsfynydd station were raised in November at a meeting of the station's

been leaked to the Guardian. Minute 508b reveals staff concern at management cuts in the numbers of hours worked, and safety at the station.

The staff representatives said that "as the lost man hours had not been replaced by an increase in staff, a decline in safety was already evident". Examples, the staff said, included a reduction in the sampling of asbestos and tanks containing radioactive liquid remaining unemptied.

"In view of the hostility of the public and the media to

for concern. Yesterday the Central Electricity Generating Board added: "We have to make the optimum use of our manpower and minimise overtime. This does not in any way prejudice our commitment to safety."

On February 12 the board will shut down the No. 1 reactor at the 22-year-old station and switch off the six giant fans which drive cooling gas around the core, in order to prove the reactor's safety under those conditions. The

Thomas (Plaid Cymru, Meirionnydd Nant Conwy) that the test would be monitored by the inspectorate, and would only be carried out when the reactor was shut down and all automatic safety systems were in operation.

The Gwynedd County Council public protection committee yesterday demanded that the experiment be abandoned. The council's chief executive, Mr Ioan Bowen, has asked the board if it would be prepared to compensation for rivers polluted by industrial waste, for water sources adulterated by pesticides and for children's brains addled by lead and food additives! Who knows where it would end? People might even start whingeing about the 5,500 people killed on this country's roads every year, and if Waldegrave and his ilk start doling out compensation for the effect roads have on our lives, it really would be the beginning of the end as we know it!

15 April 1987

20 THINGS YOU DON'T KNOW ABOUT THE POTTY PYTHONS

JOHN CLEESE TERRY JONES ERIC IDLE GRAHAM CHAPMAN

A WHOLE new generation is laughing at the zany antics of the Monty Python team.

It's nearly 20 years since John Cleese, Eric Idle, Terry Jones, Michael Palin and Graham Chapman shot to fame in Monty Python's Flying Circus.

And comedy classics like the Ministry of Silly Walks and the dead parrot sketch still set TV audiences giggling.

They're back on the box tonight (BBC 1, 10.30pm) but did you know that...

Palin aims to track down Yeti!

By TIM EWBANK and HENRIETTA KNIGHT

1 Chapman, 46, was an alcoholic one day and admits he nearly drank himself to death.

Four days after he quit booze he had a fit which scared him off drink for ever.

2 Chapman, who lives in Highgate, North London, was one of the first big TV stars to reveal that he was gay.

He says: "People tried blackmailing me but it was never successful. I just phoned the police."

3 He once invited 200 visitors to a Swansea art exhibition then pelted them with dead fish, saying it was in keeping with the art on show.

4 Chapman is the son of a police chief inspector, is a qualified doctor and his hobby is mountaineering.

5 Terry Jones, best known for his Dirty Vicar and Nude Organist skits, is the quiet member of the team.

He lives with his scientist wife Alison, daughter Samantha, 12, and son Bill, nine, in a rambling house in Camberwell, South London. He does all the cooking—his speciality is mayonnaise.

6 Jones, a pacifist, often speaks at anti-nuclear rallies. He is a big investor in the anarchic magazine Vole. His Citroen car has "Vote Ecology" stickers on it.

He says: "I sent back my American Express card because I didn't like their tone. There's something wrong about glossy leaflets inviting families to get in debt."

7 He had an interest in a 12th century brewery in Kington, Herefordshire, where they used to make 1,000 pints of Penrhos Bitter a week.

8 Born in Colwyn Bay, North Wales in 1942, Jones moved to Claygate, Surrey with his family when he was seven.

He says: "I remember my grandmother asking if I wanted more pudding. I passed her my table mat and she poured custard all over it. I thought it was hysterical."

9 Jones studied at the Royal Academy and says he spent three years painting ten-foot long stripes on canvas.

"I don't know why I did it, it was a complete waste of time," he says. "I wouldn't be seen dead with it on my wall."

10 When he was hypnotised on telly five years ago he broke down in tears and confessed he thought he had been a 14th century peasant in a former life.

11 Last year Eric Idle, 46, fulfilled his ambition to be an opera singer when he played Ko-Ko, the Lord High Executioner in the English National Opera Company's production of The Mikado.

He says: "It was one of the best times I've ever had. The part was really good. It's not often the English go loony on the stage. I suppose I'll try ballet next."

12 Idle says the most amusing hang-over from his Python days is students coming up to him in the street reciting whole sketches.

He says: "I usually say something rude which they think is a joke and fall about laughing."

13 His seven-year marriage to pretty actress Lynn Ashley, 46, ended in divorce in 1978.

Ex-Beatle George Har-rison helped him through the crisis. Eric says: "We're mates and often stay up all night talking about films."

14 In 1981 he married beautiful Playboy model Tania, 35, whom he met at a New York party.

Idle, who lives in St John's Wood, North London, says: "When my first marriage broke up the number of girls who came along were remarkable. I had a wild time. But with a girl like Tania, who needs a roving eye?"

15 He was rushed into intensive care when he fell ill after an appendix operation. He was so convinced he was dying that he made his will.

16 Michael Palin, 43, met his wife Helen on a Suffolk beach when he threw a ball at her to knock her hat off. They have lived in the same house in Gospel Oak, North London, for 18 years.

He turned their first teenage meeting into a TV play shown last year called East Of Ipswich.

17 Palin's ambition is to be an explorer. He is a Fellow of the Royal Geographical Society. Last month Yeti hunt was set to go down under when he had call it off because of work.

Palin is also chairman of Transport 2,000, a group fighting for better public transport.

18 John Cleese, 47, is really called John Cheese. His father changed the family name to Cleese when he joined the army in 1915 because he feared being teased.

19 The sixth Python, animator Terry Gilliam, lives in Highgate. His favourite place at home is the Cromwell Room dating from 1595.

The estate agent claimed it was where Cromwell decided to have King Charles I beheaded.

20 Gilliam, 46, is married to Maggie Weston, who did the make-up for his smash-hit film Brazil. They have two children—Amy, nine, and Holly, five, who appeared in Brazil.

Del's a swell

DAVID JASON
Going to college

RODNEY and Uncle Albert may not believe it, but the toff in the topper is none other than Del Boy!

Actor David Jason has temporarily given up the spiv's life for a term up at Cambridge.

He plays a grumpy college porter in a new four-part series called Porterhouse Blue, to be seen on Channel 4 in the summer. But he is back wheeling and dealing tomorrow in a repeat episode of Only Fools And Horses (BBC 1, Sunday, 9.55pm).

TWENTY THINGS YOU DIDN'T KNOW ABOUT THE *SUN*

1. The Editor of the *Sun* wears the bottoms of his pyjamas over his head and sleeps in a cupboard. He says: 'I don't know why I do it. It is a complete waste of time.'
2. The Editor of the *Sun* has six children, each one of whom is called Spot.
3. He also has a mother called Spot.
4. The Editor of the *Sun* has never been to bed with any of the Page Three Girls!
5. You may be wondering how I am able to divulge these startling revelations about the *Sun*?
6. Well, last Saturday, the *Sun* printed what purported to be an article about the Monty Python team, entitled: TWENTY THINGS YOU DIDN'T KNOW ABOUT THE POTTY PYTHONS.
7. Among these things were several things about myself which I certainly didn't know about.
8. The *Sun* claimed, for example, that I have a daughter called Samantha. I do not have a daughter called Samantha.
9. The *Sun* also claimed I often speak at anti-nuclear rallies. I have never spoken at a CND rally, and only once, very briefly, said something at an anti-nuclear power rally.
10. The *Sun* also said I have a Citroën car which has VOTE ECOLOGY stickers on it. I have never had a Citroën car, and the car that I do have has no stickers.
11. The *Sun* further stated as follows: 'Jones studied at the Royal Academy, and says he spent three years painting

ten-foot-long stripes on canvas. "I don't know why I did it, it was a complete waste of time," he says. "I wouldn't be seen dead with it on my wall."'

I suppose it is possible that I am suffering from total amnesia about three years of my life, but to the best of my knowledge I never went to any art school – let alone the Royal Academy. Nor have I ever painted a ten-foot stripe, let alone claimed that I didn't know why I did it. Now, to suggest that I actually claimed not to know why I spent three years of my life doing something that I didn't do in the first place seems to me to be dangerously close to defamation. It certainly makes me look soft in the head.

12. So to get back to the TWENTY THINGS YOU DIDN'T KNOW ABOUT THE *SUN*.

13. The Editor of the *Sun*'s cousin is called Clive. He lives in Dorking, where he breeds dingbats.

14. The Editor of the *Sun* feels he can print anything he wants to print about anybody, true or untrue, as long as it's not defamatory.

15. 98 per cent of the *Sun*'s readers are frequently unable to distinguish fact from fiction.

16. 98 per cent of the *Sun*'s editorial staff are frequently unable to distinguish fact from fiction.

17. 98 per cent of the Editor of the *Sun*'s brain is frequently on holiday in Majorca.

18. The *Sun* once actually printed a piece of accurate information (by mistake).

19. The *Sun* used to be a socialist newspaper.

20. The present owner of the *Sun* is an Australian with a keen sense of fair-play and a deep desire to see Neil Kinnock returned as Prime Minister at the next election, as well as being deeply committed to the truth and to seeing a return to decent standards of journalism in this country.

22 April 1987

A THATCHER ALPHABET

Teaching unions wary of plans to impose uniform standards

Baker sets out new national curriculum

Of course, as anyone who reads the *Daily Telegraph* can tell you, our classrooms are dominated by teachers who are either Marxist-Leninists or card-carrying members of the Red Army Faction. And it is, perhaps, one of the blackest marks against Mrs Thatcher's government that she has failed to uproot them all from our schools.

She has done her best to alienate teachers from public opinion, by persuading them to strike for the first time in their history, and she has waged a remarkably successful campaign to lower their morale to a point where a good many of them are by now thoroughly ashamed of still being teachers. She has even deprived them of resources and materials in an attempt to starve the trouble-makers out. And yet, despite it all, there are *still* teachers in charge of our children today who may vote other than Tory at the next election! Incredible, isn't it?

Under these circumstances, it can't be any surprise to anyone that the government has finally been forced to impose what it calls a 'National Curriculum' on our schools. This means that instead of allowing irresponsible and revolutionary teachers to decide what to teach their pupils, the government decides for them.

And why not? The government (I'm sorry, I mean Mr Norman Tebbit, who, as Chairman of the Conservative Party, is of course completely independent of the government) now tells the BBC what it should include in its newscasts, so why not start getting public thinking into line right from the nursery?

To help in this great endeavour, I'd like to offer up a small contribution of my own. This is a politically correct Alphabet for compulsory use in infant schools, which is designed to instil the high values of the Prime Minister into the minds of our children even as they learn to read.

I'm not sure that some of it couldn't be improved somewhat, but I hope that readers will write in with their own suggestions or even complete alphabets. The Editor of the *Guardian* tells me he is prepared to offer, as a prize for the best alphabet, a signed photograph of our Leader.

A THATCHER ALPHABET

A for her ABILITY
    (to prove black is white),

B for her BELIEF
    (that she's always right).

C for her CARING
    (that the affluent thrive),

D for her DARING
    (to protect MI5).

E for her ENERGY
    (which is nuclear-powered),

F for the FALL-OUT
    (with which we are showered).

G for her GENEROSITY
    (when not sparing the rod),

H for her HUMBLENESS
    (shown only to God).

I for her INTELLIGENCE
    (at GCHQ),

J for her JUSTICE
　　　(reserved for the few).

K for her KNOWLEDGE
　　　(of the Westland Affair),

L for her LOVE
　　　(of a bald millionaire).

M for her MAJESTY
　　　(plain as her nose),

N for her NOBILITY
　　　(whose titles she chose).

O for her OPENNESS
　　　(to Jimmy Young),

P for her POLITICS
　　　(she reads in the *Sun*).

Q for the QUANDARY
　　　(that she's never been in),

R for her REALISM
　　　(when her underlings sin).

S for the SINCERITY
　　　(with which she hates coal),

T for her TACT
　　　(counting those on the dole).

U for her UNDERSTANDING
　　　(of what the police need),

V for her VISION
　　　(of a world built on greed).

W for her WILL
　　　(to see money well spent),

X for the VOTES
　　　(that she won't get in Brent).

Y for her YOUTH
　　　(and their employment schemes),

Z for her ZEST
　　　(in crushing their dreams).

29 April 1987

AID FOR THE CONTRAS

I don't know whether you've been following the latest revelations by Bob 'Watergate' Woodward about CIA involvement in Nicaragua, but it's certainly been causing a stir in Washington. The immediate result is that it's becoming increasingly difficult for the American government to get urgently needed aid to the Contras for their fight against the so-called 'Sandinista' government of Nicaragua. So I am taking this opportunity to appeal to *you* to support them.

Nicaragua is a little country, just over half the size of Britain, squashed in between Honduras and Costa Rica. Its population is roughly a quarter that of London and is mainly occupied with agriculture. Now, the snag is that all over Nicaragua there are people who have a slightly different political philosophy from Nancy Reagan. Indeed, there are so many of them who have a slightly different political philosophy from Nancy Reagan that, at the last general election, they actually voted in a government which also has a slightly different political philosophy from Nancy Reagan.

Now, of course, this is a state of affairs that no responsible American administration could allow to flourish – unchecked – on its own doorstep. After all, Managua (the capital) is almost as close to Washington as Addis Ababa is

White House wants contra aid doubled

BOB WOODWARD

President makes his wife 'national heroine' for work on drug abuse

Reagan presses home attack on Sandinistas

VEIL:
The Secret
Wars of the
CIA 1981–1987

SIMON & SCHUSTER

Reagan's authority suffers in US foreign policy fight

Congress ready for showdown on aid to Nicaraguan rebels

Doubt on aid for contras

From Maurice Walsh
in Managua

The Reagan Administration's decision to request $70 million for the Nicaraguan contras is a predictable hindrance to the prospects for the fragile peace...

to London! And if the British government were to allow the
Ethiopians to go around proclaiming a political philosophy
as slightly different from Margaret Thatcher's as Daniel
Ortega's is from Nancy Reagan's – well! Where would our
credibility on the world stage be?

Of course, the Ethiopians speak a very obscure language
called Amharic, so (fortunately) we can't actually understand what any of them are proclaiming in the first place –
let alone grasp what their political philosophy is – but that's
not the point. The point is that the American government
simply cannot allow the Nicaraguans to go around saying
things like: 'The land belongs to those who work on it'! For
a kick-off, the land they're talking about is actually part of
America . . . well the American continent anyway . . .
And I mean, it's bad enough when the Cubans start saying
that sort of thing, but at least they're separated from the
Freest Country In The World by a bit of water. But Daniel
Ortega and his cronies are actually standing right there on
the very same landmass as Ollie North and Doris Day –
cheeking Nancy Reagan to her face, as it were, along with
her ideals *and* aspirations for the Future of Mankind!

So you see how crucial it is to keep funds and arms
flowing to the brave men of the Contras who – for nothing
more than a wage-packet – are prepared to devote themselves to killing anybody in Nicaragua who shows a lack of
respect for the First Lady of the United States. Their
heroism *demands* our support. I have heard of one Contra
Freedom Fighter who burnt his fingers badly while setting
fire to a farm (which, incidentally, contained an entire
family who disagreed with Nancy Reagan's economic
theories). Another fellow I know of sprained *both* ankles
while running away from a school bus he'd just blown up.
I was also told of yet another who was actually pelted
with stones by a crowd of bigots, after he'd executed a
Nicaraguan who not only hadn't agreed with Nancy
Reagan's concept of self-help but had actually called her

husband 'a stupid old bat'! The reaction of the crowd who pelted him was particularly hard to understand, since the fellow who got shot was easily over eleven years old and clearly knew what he was talking about.

In short, the Future of the Free World, the CIA and even the right to buy and sell Coca-Cola itself depends on this vital struggle in Latin America. The brave, dedicated men of the Contras need our support urgently. So *please* send any money (or weapons if you can spare them) direct to:

> **The Contras,**
> **c/o Nancy Reagan,**
> **The White House,**
> **Washington, D C,**
> **USA**

(For a quicker delivery mark the envelope: FROM IRAN.)

7 October 1987

THE ZEEBRUGGE INQUIRY

I'm jolly relieved to see those Townsend Thoresen people got away with it at the Zeebrugge disaster inquiry. The coroner said they were 'too remote to be held criminally responsible'.

Now this legal principle of 'remoteness' is very good news. You see, I was planning a bank robbery (some time next month) and I'd been intending to go along and watch, but now, in view of coroner Richard Sturt's principle of 'remoteness', I realize I'd be better off keeping well out of it. If I stay safe at home in – say – Gerrards Cross or Chalfont St Giles, while the bank is being robbed in – say – Folkestone or Dover, I'll be legally in the clear.

I suppose I also ought to form myself into a proper limited company – just to make sure I'm *really* protected from the law. Moreover, if anything goes wrong, I can always change the name. Supposing I started off as: Thoresen Bank Robberies plc. I could change it to: Townsend Bank Clearances or even: P & O European Vault Extractions Ltd.

The beauty of the whole thing is that even if somebody gets killed, my company will now be legally 'too remote to be held criminally responsible', since I will only be organizing the enterprise and not actually carrying it out.

Of course, if they want to hang any of my operatives, there won't be much I can do about it, but then it's pretty

Two crewmen could face prosecution

Zeebrugge deaths were unlawful says inquest jury

By Paul Brown

Criminal charges against two members of the Herald of Free Enterprise crew are to be considered by the Director of Public Prosecutions following an inquest jury's verdict yesterday that 187 of the 188 victims of the Zeebrugge disaster were unlawfully killed.

so sorry for the captain and the crew. I think they have suffered enough.

"They were on it as we were and I know what they went through.

"Something went wrong that night, but we do not feel they were to blame."

Mr Sturt had offered the positive verdict

Salvage workers on the side of the Herald of Free Enterprise yesterday as the ferry was righted outside Zeebrugge harbour

Zeebrugge's truth finds cold harbour

60 bodies are recovered from righted Herald

well understood in bank-robbing circles that the chaps on the spot have to carry the can. I imagine it's the same in the ferry business – at least it is now.

21

ATTACKS OF OPINION

In future, if any company invests in badly designed ships that have a tendency to capsize when they get even a couple of feet of water in them, then it will be understood that the captain will be responsible when they do. After all, every captain knows that safety *has* to take a back seat, when the priority is to get the cars on and off more quickly.

For let us never forget that Townsend Thoresen – I'm sorry, I mean P & O European Ferries – are not in the business of molly-coddling rowdy tourists. They are in the business, first and foremost, of making profits. That was the whole point of denationalizing the Channel ferry operation: to replace the comfortable apathy of state-control with its woolly-minded ideas of safety before profits – with good, healthy competition.

Now, in any healthy, competitive enterprise there are bound to be a few casualties, and – in this case – there just happened to be 188 of them. But that's no justification for hounding the innocent proprietors of the company who, for all I know, were sitting innocently in their homes in Gerrards Cross or Chalfont St Giles, innocently sipping gin and tonics on the night in question. Much better to make an example of the men on the spot, who went through the ordeal and who were so clearly guilty of operating the badly designed ships and inadequate safety systems that the company supplied them with.

Besides, if we start pointing the finger at remote company executives, there's no knowing where it may end! Before you know where you are, people will be trying to blame the Distillers Company for the thalidomide tragedy or British Nuclear Fuels for the children who have died of leukaemia in Seascale. No. Better just to execute the men on the spot, like we do in bank-robbing.

Incidentally, if anyone has a list of banks they think may be particularly worth robbing at the moment, I'd be very grateful to hear from them.

14 October 1987

FIJI

Coup in Fiji

THE ARMY seized power in a coup yesterday in the South Pacific island state of Fiji.

The troops, indigenous Fijians took over from the government of Mr Timoci Bavadra, which was dominated by ethnic make up

My Jack Russell has some high-powered Corgi friends who came round the other day with a letter purporting to be from the Queen to Mrs Thatcher. I tell you this because I think it best to reveal my sources straight away, and save the police the expense and trouble of breaking in and ransacking my office. Here is the letter.

Dear Mrs Thatcher,

I can't understand why you haven't sent the Task Force to Fiji yet. I know it's a lot further away than the Falklands, but the weather's much pleasanter there, and the issue is just as clear-cut. In the Falklands you said we were fighting an unpleasant military dictatorship which sought to supplant me as Head of State. That's exactly what's happened in Fiji.

So why no action? Why no rousing patriotic speeches? And why aren't any of your newspapers running a few UP YOURS, RABUKA! headlines? It only takes a phone call . . .

Quite frankly, I'm mystified. I know you're not scared of Col. Rabuka, because you're not scared of anyone (not even Roy Hattersley!). And in any case, the Royal Fiji Military Force is only 2,600 – well! That's little more than five *Belgrano*-fulls! E - A - S - Y!

23

Of course, I agree with you when you said, at the Commonwealth Prime Ministers' Conference last week, that what is important is the democratic right of the people of Fiji. But I couldn't quite follow your logic when you said that this was best served by not upsetting the gentleman who had just ousted their democratically elected government and told me to get knotted!

Quite honestly, Margaret, Col. Rabuka is, in my book, a traitor, and I make no bones about that . . .

Unfortunately the next bit of the letter is a bit gnawed-away for some reason. However, it continues some paragraphs further on:

You told me privately that the Fijians have only got themselves to blame, because they went and voted in a Labour government and (what's worse) a Labour government committed to a nuclear-free Pacific.

Now, of course, it goes without saying that *nobody* wants a Labour government (except, I suppose, for the majority of Fijians), but that's no reason for letting someone like Rabuka get away with bare-faced treason.

You also told me in private that your American friends are so jumpy about the whole idea of a nuclear-free Pacific (where they wouldn't be able to dock their nuclear warships and so on) that they can't be held responsible for any actions they might take in countries like Fiji that adopt such loony-left policies.

Are you really saying that if you sent in the Task Force, like you did in the Falklands, instead of the Argies we'd find ourselves up against the Americans?

Well, if it comes to that, so be it! I've every confidence in you, Mrs T., as the best wartime leader we've had since the War – ever since I saw those photographs of you in your combat jacket . . . or was it that nice Mr Heseltine?

Please let me know by return that you have dispatched the Fleet.

Yours sincerely

E.R.

PS How did you enjoy the bag of bones I sent round the other week?

Personally, I think the PS casts a little doubt on the authenticity of the whole letter, but on the other hand, I can't see why a bunch of Corgis would be interested enough in Fiji to bother forging anything. Come to think of it, I can't think why the Americans are that interested in Fiji either – and yet my dog assures me they are.

21 October 1987

POWER TO THE PEOPLE

I don't see why anyone should be so up in arms about the new Bill to curb trade union powers. After all, it only says that all trade unions must hold a secret ballot on whether or not to strike, and that whatever the result nobody needs to take any notice of it.

This is exactly the same principle that the late Sir David Owen invoked when the majority of the SDP voted to merge with the Liberal Party. Sir David simply pointed out that the majority who voted to merge could, while those who voted not to needn't.

It's a principle I should very much like to see extended to general elections. No matter which party the majority votes for, nobody should be compelled to take any notice of the result. If you didn't vote for a Conservative government, you shouldn't be compelled to have one. Those who voted Labour could have a Labour government, and those who voted Liberal could have an SDP one.

It's what Norman Fowler, the Employment Secretary, calls giving people 'protection from the abuse of power and the rights they are entitled to expect in a free society'. Of course, he was only thinking about trade union members, but the wider application of the principle is clear. We need to give the government of this country back to the people.

If it is wrong for a trade unionist to be forced to do

something he doesn't want to simply because the majority have voted for it, why should any individual be forced to do anything he didn't vote for?

I, myself, for example, didn't vote for stopping at red traffic lights at the last election. So why shouldn't I have the freedom to go on red lights and stop at green ones, if that's what I choose to do?

I also didn't vote for returning library books on time, and now I have high hopes that Mr Fowler will set up a £1.2 million a year fund to enable me to take my library to court if it tries to fine me for returning books late – just as he is proposing for trade unionists who feel like taking their unions to court.

FRIDAY, 23 OCTOBER, 1987 –

Maggie's new curb on union power

by Richard Littlejohn

THE BILL to curb trades union power further and strengthen the rights of individual workers was published by the Government today.

It will be law by next summer and will outlaw the closed shop, give everyone the right to work regardless of an official strike, and force all union leaders to face election by secret ballot.

The new measures close loopholes in previous Acts and are the fourth phase of Tory plans "to give the unions back to their members."

A new Commissioner will be created to help workers take their own union to court. In future no one will have to belong to a union to keep a job.

It will become illegal to take industrial action to enforce a closed shop, even if the majority of staff want one.

No one will be forced to take part in a strike against their will. Unions will be prevented from disciplining any member for crossing picket lines.

Anyone who is disciplined will be entitled to compensation.

Employment Secretary Norman Fowler said today: "We must ensure union members have protection from abuse of power and the rights they are entitled to expect in a free society."

The Bill also makes all members of a union's national executive face election by secret postal ballot, which must be supervised by an independent outside organisation such as the Electoral Reform Society.

Strict new controls on the use of trade union funds will be introduced next summer.

Elections

The way in which money was shuffled around Europe to evade the courts during the miners' strike has convinced Ministers that union leaders should be prevented from dealing with money unlawfully.

In future union leaders will become personally liable for their actions. The Government believes that the threat of losing his home would be a powerful incentive to anyone to remain within the law.

Unions will be banned from indemnifying officials or paying their fines—whether for contempt of court or picket line violence.

Other unions will be prevented from providing financial assistance to those whose funds have been seized by the courts.

Union members would have the right to inspect the books accompanied by a qualified accountant.

It's all a question of giving more power to the individual – as Mr Fowler says. Of course, some would say that this is precisely what trade unions were formed to do in the first place.

During the Industrial Revolution, individuals found themselves powerless when employers asked them to work long, unsocial hours for starvation wages. If they refused they were fired, and somebody else got the job. The idea of everybody refusing to do the job unless conditions were improved was supposed to be a way of giving power to the individual – power against employers who sought to exploit him or her.

Nowadays, of course, things are totally different. It is a measure of the almost unbelievable way in which human nature has changed for the better that Mr Fowler can once again talk of returning some of those ancient freedoms that we have lost over the last century: the freedom not to do what we don't vote for, the freedom to ignore the needs of our fellows, the freedom to have no say in how our employers treat us, the freedom to be fired, the freedom to starve and the freedom not to be able to do anything about any of it.

28 October 1987

Steps along the road to union serfdom

TRADE unions, even now regarded by the Government as unique and privileged, and in Thatcherite philosophy as still embodying all that is wrong with collectivism, will soon be no more than friendly societies, the role of their members strictly limited to the particular enterprise for which they are working.

That prediction was made last night by Lord Wedderburn professor of commercial law the London School of Econ ics and doyen of this industrial relations

past measures and cul posals with extracts works of Friedrich guru once describ Thatcher as supreme."

TERRORISTS

My Gran asked me why they allowed Mr Adolfo Calero, the leader of the Nicaraguan Contras, to visit the House of Commons last week, give interviews on the radio and speak at the Royal Institute of International Affairs, when everyone knows his organization kills men and women and blows up schoolchildren by the busful, in order to persuade other Nicaraguans not to support their democratically elected government. Why didn't they arrest him at the airport, she demanded, or deport him, like they do her?

I told my Gran to mind her own business, and to get on with her molotov cocktails, but nevertheless I looked up the word 'terrorist' in the *Dictionary of Things People Never Mention*, and discovered something nobody had ever mentioned to me. According to the *DTPNM*, a 'terrorist' is not a 'terrorist' simply because he goes round killing people for political ends. It all depends on the political ends in question, and on how keen you are on the people he is terrorizing.

For example, if my Gran blows up the Labour Party HQ because, as she claims, they've 'gone soft on capitalism', it would be an act of terrorism only if both Mr Reagan and Mrs Thatcher were really enthusiastic about the political aspirations of Neil Kinnock and his friends. Otherwise it's just mass murder.

This explains why, according to the *Dictionary of Things People Never Mention*, the CIA is not a terrorist organization, and why, when a CIA bomb blows up seventy-three passers-by in Beirut, it is not an act of terrorism but of anti-terrorism.

Similarly, when the CIA masterminded the bombing and killing of the democratically elected President of Chile some years ago, that was not an act of terrorism either, because, as everyone knows, President Allende was a communist, and you cannot terrorize a communist. It's a contradiction in terms.

Now, both Mrs Thatcher and Mr Reagan are known to sympathize deeply with the political aspirations of Mr Calero's colleagues, but they do not like the political aspirations of the democratically elected government of Nicaragua one little bit. So, as the associate of murderers rather than terrorists, Mr Calero ought to be free to come and go in the House of Commons – just as long, that is, as he isn't planning to become some Labour MP's research assistant.*

Mr Bowen Wells, the Conservative MP for Hertford and Stortford, put the whole matter very succinctly when he said that the democratically elected government of Nicaragua has 'had representatives visiting at the invitation of Labour MPs', and so it is only right that Mr Calero should be admitted to put 'the contrary point of view'. If that point of view is that Nicaraguans should be dissuaded from supporting their democratically elected government by having their children blown up on their way to school, then he is entitled to his opinion. It still does not make him a terrorist . . . which is certainly more than you can say for my Gran.

4 November 1987

* In 1987 Ronan Bennett, the research assistant of Jeremy Corbyn, MP (Islington North), found his House of Commons pass suspended because he had been *cleared* of two serious charges in the past.

THE OZONE LAYER

Ozone hole warning

From Mark Tran in Washington

After a six-week expedition in Antarctica, scientists have tentatively concluded that man-made chemicals have contributed to a depletion of the ozone layer, which shields earth from harmful ultra-violet rays.

The scientific team found that the ozone layer over Antarctica dwindled last month to the lowest level sin~ ~ing con~

The end of the human race cannot be put before the interests of aerosol manufacturers. This important decision was reached by the top brains of twenty-four countries in Montreal this September.

It was an historic decision, because, for the first time, governments from all over the world put aside political and national differences to ensure that the threat of global pollution does not bring disaster on the multinational companies which are causing it.

In 1985 a hole the size of the United States appeared in the ozone layer above the Antarctic. Without the ozone layer, more UV-B rays from the sun penetrate the atmosphere with various inconvenient results, such as: a massive increase in skin cancers, reduced crop productivity, depletion of fish stocks, and climate changes resulting in floods and famine and, for all I know, another Republican Senate.

The scientists rushed to the conclusion, over the next few years, that the depletion of the ozone layer was due to chemicals known as chlorofluorocarbons, or CFCs, which are used in such things as aerosols, hamburger packaging and refrigerators.

The cooler heads of such companies as ICI, DuPont, Hoechst and Atochem (who, incidentally, make CFCs) advised caution, until it could be proved beyond all reasonable doubt that global extinction was at hand and they had developed a cheaper alternative. But moderation, I'm afraid, lost the day. Hence the Montreal conference.

Most scientists agree that a reduction of 85 per cent in CFC emissions is needed immediately – just to stabilize conditions. In Montreal, however, the top brains from twenty-four countries (aided, I suppose, by advisers from ICI, DuPont, Hoechst and Atochem) decided on a reduction of only 50 per cent, and then not until 1998. Moreover, they were talking only about *consumption* of CFCs. If you read the fine print, you'll find that they've actually agreed to let the big companies increase their *production* of CFCs until 1990.

I'm sorry, I'd better repeat that. Faced with the extinction of the human race by depletion of the ozone layer owing to the manufacture of CFCs, the top brains of twenty-four countries agreed to *increase* the production of CFCs.

Ultimately a decrease is to be achieved by 1999, but then only by 35 per cent – not 50 per cent. Meanwhile, exports to the Third World are to be stepped up, presumably on the principle that if the ozone layer does finally go, at least we can blame it on people with unpronounceable names.

It is a brilliant formulation. The environmentalists are happy because nobody likes to seem ungrateful. The manufacturers of CFCs are happy, because they can go on doing what they were doing. The governments of the twenty-four countries are happy, because they will be seen to be doing more than they are.

It's true that the hole in the ozone layer will go on getting

35

bigger and bigger, until our children's children will think no more of a cancer in their skin than of grazing their knee, and their yardstick of good health will be to have a nose like Ronald Reagan's. But who cares?

As the Secretary of the Interior of the United States put it: so what if the ozone layer does go? We'll all just have to wear hats, dark glasses and barrier cream whenever we go out of doors.

What may seem like a huge problem can just vanish into thin air, when you've got the kind of brain that guides the destinies of so many countries on this earth – at least twenty-four of them.

11 November 1987

A SUGGESTION

I was sitting on the loo the other day, thinking about self-regulation, when a brilliant thought struck me. Since the police are always investigating complaints against themselves, as do doctors, lawyers, stockbrokers and the nuclear power industry, why not allow criminals to do the same?

A watch-dog committee of professional criminals with a proven track-record would be both logical and beneficial. It is patently absurd to allow amateurs such as jurors, barristers, magistrates and judges, who (with a few honourable exceptions) have little first-hand experience of committing crimes, to adjudicate over some of the most enterprising and resourceful practitioners at work in this country today.

Far better to leave it to the professionals. Let them be the judge of who is or who is not a criminal. Leave it to men who know what it's like to be out there in the real world of free enterprise, and who understand the goals and pitfalls, the rewards and punishments of their chosen trade.

Some people, I know, may object to this idea on the grounds that when the police, the lawyers, the doctors, the stockbrokers and the nuclear power industry investigate complaints against themselves, ninety-nine times out of a hundred they also exonerate themselves, and while a 1 per cent conviction rate is fine as far as the police, lawyers, doctors, stockbrokers and the nuclear power industry are concerned, it is rather less satisfactory when it's a question of muggers, bank-robbers and unilateral disarmers. But I would suggest that, in practice, all sorts of benefits would accrue to a self-regulating criminal profession.

I THINK I'D BETTER INVESTIGATE MYSELF

Firstly, a conviction rate of 1 per cent would do wonders for our overcrowded prisons. Gaols would be emptied overnight, and could then be turned into privatized rest-homes for the elderly, or else into labour camps for school-leavers.

Secondly, the government would be able to claim a startling reduction in the crime rate. They could easily assert that this was the direct result of their policy of widening the gap between rich and poor, thus giving the lie to all those do-gooding social theorists who . . . But I digress.

Thirdly, the project would relieve the police of some of the most tedious and time-consuming work which they undertake, and leave them free to get on with doing the things that they do well – such as investigating complaints against themselves or stopping black men in cars.

One other objection may be raised, and that is that it might be dangerous to allow such a large proportion of the criminal population to run free. But I wonder? The murder rate, for example, probably compares pretty favourably with the number of people who die in hospital through the mistakes or neglect of the medical profession. And if you throw in those who are killed in police custody or in car crashes involving police cars, the professional killers probably score considerably less.

And when it comes to the nuclear power industry – well! There certainly aren't many criminals who pose a threat to whole continents, or who can claim to have destroyed miles of Cumbrian coastline, wiped out half the sheep farms of Wales and Scotland and poisoned the entire reindeer herds of Lapland!

No, criminals, by and large, have a far better record. Why not give them the chance to be their own judge and jury like we do with everyone else?

18 November 1987

ANTI WOMEN VEHICLE

OPO

Apart from ignoring fire risks, nothing has saved London Regional Transport more money than the move to One Person Operated buses and trains. In fact, the move has proved so successful that, I understand, Mrs Thatcher is considering extending the principle to her own government.

In practice, of course, she already does run an OPO (One Person Operated) Cabinet, but a more thorough-going One Person Operated government would provide staggering savings for the taxpayer.

After all, what is the point of doling out £32,208 for a Secretary of State for Defence, or £45,000 for a Kenneth Baker in Education, when everyone knows that all the decisions are taken by the Prime Minister anyway? The same goes for the £62,100 we forked out last year for Lord Young, just so he could put 'Secretary of State for Employment' on his notepaper.

No. It is high time Mrs Thatcher swept away the whole expensive charade.

In fact, come to think of it, the entire parliamentary process is ridiculously over-staffed as it is. I mean, what *is* the point of all those MPs sitting in the House of Commons, day after day, debating whether or not to pass legislation that *they* know and *we* know Mrs T. has already decided on?

Far better to face up to reality and do away with the lot of them. After all, each MP may earn only a nominal £17,702 a year, but they can also claim expenses of up to £20,562, of which £7,351 is tax-free! That means an MP's real take-home pay is around £41,264 – and there are 650 of them! The whole pantomime is therefore costing the British taxpayer something like £26 million – and that's not including all their secretaries, researchers, caterers and secret policemen. Last year, MPs' travel expenses *alone* kissed goodbye to a cool £4 million!

Yet another OPO bus tragedy

Another OPO bus tragedy has forced a coroner into writing to LRT about the safety of the bus doors for a second time.

A leaner, more competitive parliamentary process would only add another 650 – or, rather, 649 – to the dole queue. And even this could probably be massaged down to a respectable forty or fifty, if we don't count the women or those who fill in their dole forms incorrectly.

Another beauty of the scheme is that it would free one of London's most attractive and historic sites for redevelopment. Alternatively, the Houses of Parliament could be turned into the Prime Minister's official residence – much more fitting for the ruler of the Tenth Greatest Nation in the World* than that poky Downing Street.

* Assessed by the L L R T method (Length of Longest Railway Tunnel).

I know there are those who harbour doubts about OPO. They claim that old ladies have got trapped in train doors and been dragged down the line from Bedford to St Pancras before anyone noticed. They assert that OPO buses clog up London's streets because it takes so long for passengers to get on, and that the strain on drivers is already showing up in the increasing numbers of accidents due to driver error.

But what are a few accidents compared to savings on this scale?

Besides, it wouldn't be the first time Mrs T. has swept away centuries of representative tradition. If she could do it with the GLC, she can do it with central government. Go for it, Maggie!

25 November 1987

ADVERTISING NUCLEAR POWER

You may have wondered why the Central Electricity Generating Board is allowed to run glossy commercials on TV telling us how cheap, safe and clean nuclear power is, when Greenpeace were banned from putting out commercials saying the opposite.

The answer is, quite simply, because one set of statements is true and the other false. The Independent Broadcasting Authority clearly takes the view that it is unethical for TV commercials to seek to persuade the public that something is true if it actually *is* true.

Nuclear fear

NUCLEAR pollution is worrying tourist chiefs in Cumbria and the Lake District after hotels blamed a decrease in business on the publicity about Chernobyl and Sellafield.

Nuclear power is not cheap. Even the Chairman of the CEGB, Lord Marshall, has finally admitted that. It's actually the most expensive source of electricity there is – if you use normal accounting techniques rather than the Paul Daniels School of Accountancy methods, favoured by the CEGB.

Nor is nuclear power safe. As if Chernobyl wasn't enough, last month the National Radiological Protection Board admitted that the current levels of radiation to which the public may be exposed are three times too high!

As for being clean – well! Who swims in the Irish Sea any more? Everything Prince Charles said about the North Sea is true about the Irish Sea with radioactive knobs on.

Another criterion which the IBA apparently applies to its TV commercials is that they should never promote anything that is useful, necessary or that people actually want. And here, once again, nuclear power is well up to advertising standards.

Chernobyl effects 'may last 30 years'

Many people outside the nuclear industry assume that nuclear power is useful, because they mistakenly believe that nuclear power generates electricity. Of course, it doesn't. The electricity is generated by steam-driven turbines. Nuclear power is simply another way of heating the water to make the steam. It's still good old-fashioned Victorian technology with a bit of twentieth-century violence thrown in – rather like exploding an atom bomb to boil a kettle, and I don't think you can say that is exactly 'useful'. It certainly isn't necessary, because there are so many other ways of boiling kettles . . . most of which are more sensible, and all of which are cheaper.

And as for whether or not anybody actually wants nuclear power . . . good gracious! Even the electricity industry itself doesn't want it – not if it's got to pay for it – and it looks as if poor old Cecil Parkinson (who is head prefect in charge of privatizing electricity) is jolly well going to have to make nuclear power compulsory.

So why does the CEGB go on producing the glossy ads? The answer is that Cecil has been told on no account must the electricity industry ever have to rely on coal again (even if it *is* cheaper), for fear the miners might once more hold the nation's electricity to ransom, as they did back in the dark, wet days of Mr Heath.

Sellafield leukaemia risk confirmed

Far better to hand the country over to the nuclear engineers. Far better that seas should be destroyed, that Cumbria should be full of children dying from leukaemia. Far better for the CEGB to spend millions of the taxpayers' money on TV commercials promoting lies that it doesn't even believe itself about nuclear power.

After all, the only way in which nuclear power can be said to be cheap, safe and clean is in *political* terms, and that, I suppose, is all that really matters in this country today.

2 December 1987

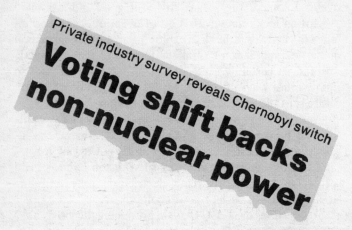

Private industry survey reveals Chernobyl switch

Voting shift backs non-nuclear power

SPYCATCHER

Futile and silly for publication ban to continue

The *Spycatcher* affair raises some uncomfortable questions about the nature of our democracy, so I'm jolly relieved to see the government using its chief law officer to stop the BBC discussing it or anything remotely connected with MI5 or MI6. As the Attorney-General's counsel put it: 'Those who work for the secret service should not speak or write about their work, and if they do seek to do so the media should not seek to assist them by publishing what they say.'

Absolutely!

If – for example – thirty officers in MI5 didn't like the government that the majority of their fellow-countrymen had voted into power, and consequently set about de-stabilizing that government, nobody – repeat – nobody should ever know anything about it.

Blanket ban sought on press spy stories

I mean supposing – just supposing – these thirty officers in MI5 actually succeeded in getting rid of a government like – for example – Harold Wilson's, and supposing – just supposing – they also managed to replace a wet leader of the opposition like – for example – Edward Heath with a strong right-wing candidate whom they preferred, and that candidate was now Prime Minister and running the country today in a way that MI5 approved of – well! It doesn't take a genius to realize that such revelations would not only be against the National Interest but against the interests of Democracy itself.

SPY
CATCHER
The Candid Autobiography of a
Senior Intelligence Officer

PETER WRIGHT
WITH PAUL GREENGRASS

VIKING

It is surely crucial to a democracy that the general public should be protected from the knowledge that its politicians are being manipulated by its own secret service. Once people begin to suspect that things like that are going on, they might well start to lose faith in the power of the ballot-box, and that would never do!

Far better that the BBC should be gagged, that the Attorney-General should lie to Parliament, and that those involved should take their secrets to the grave and – in the case of one particular ex-MI5 officer – the sooner the better!

As our present Attorney-General, Sir Patrick Something-Or-Other, put it: 'Members and former members of the security service are under a life-long obligation to the Crown.'

Now he didn't actually say what he means by 'the Crown', but he certainly doesn't mean the people of this country, nor does he mean the Queen or any of her left-wing relatives. So I assume he means the government – and not just the government of the day, but the *real* government, that goes on ruling no matter what political party is in power and despite the whims and vagaries of such things as general elections.

Democracy can work only when the true essential freedoms are safeguarded: the freedom, for example, of MI5 to do what it wants, and the freedom of politicians to wheel and deal without being subjected to public scrutiny.

So let us keep the wraps on the worm-eaten corruption that goes on behind the closed doors of Whitehall. Let us for ever seal the can of putrefying morality and naked self-interest that masquerades as political life in this country, before the rot sets in, and the people of Britain wake up to the sort of governance we are all living under.

Mark you, when Sir Patrick Whoever-He-Is claims in Parliament that he didn't know about the evil treason about to be perpetrated by the BBC until he read about it in the *Daily Telegraph*, it makes you wonder just what sort of a secret service he is getting from MI5 in the first place!

I suppose they're all too busy planning what to do if Ken Livingstone ever becomes Prime Minister.

9 December 1987

'reedom of the press is not an optional extra, but a right to be recognised'

'op judges spurn Spycatcher ban

LIGHT BLUE TOUCH PAPER AND RETIRE FROM LIFE

FOR SALE FOR A HUGE AMOUNT OF MONEY

THE INF AGREEMENT

All this euphoria over the Gorbachev–Reagan summit makes me want to throw up. Everybody is so busy hailing the proposal to get rid of 1,752 Soviet and 859 American missiles as an historic step in world something-or-other that nobody gives a monkey's fart for what it'll do to people like me.

Summit lays groundwork for Moscow cooperation

You see, ever since Mr Reagan said he'd run for President, I've been manufacturing high-grade nuclear warheads in my potting-shed. Of course, I haven't been doing it on the same scale as some of the really big boys, but I've still been able to clear a cool extra few million dollars a year pocket-money. And you can't just cut off an income like that without so much as a by your leave. One gets used to a certain standard of living, you know.

When we in the arms industry voted President Reagan into office, he promised us the earth (some would say quite literally) and, to begin with, he certainly did his level best for us. He appointed one of our number as Secretary of State – good old Al Haig, who was a Director of United Technologies, one of the biggest US military contractors. And sure enough, he bumped up the amount the government sent our way by 20 per cent!

Morale in the arms business couldn't have been higher. We knew that golden days of profit lay ahead. President Reagan's own son, Michael (who worked for a firm that supplies bits for missiles), even circulated a letter to his friends in the Defense Department, saying: now my dad's in the White House, there's going to be a lot more gravy slopping around for the arms industry, and my company wants a go with the spoon.

Reagan Jr. name-drop scandal

Other weapons manufacturers, such as myself, forked out huge amounts of money to build new plant, to establish relations with Michael Reagan's friends in the Defense Department, and to enlarge our potting-sheds. No wonder we are all now up in arms about the INF agreement – metaphorically that is, of course.

For us, perhaps the most offensive part of the whole charade has been the sight of Gorbachev and Reagan being so friendly to each other. Has Mr Reagan forgotten that to have a healthy and flourishing arms industry, you must have an enemy? How can you expect the great American public to hand over 54 cents out of every tax dollar to the military (past and present) when the so-called enemy is hailed by the President as a long-lost friend, and allowed to go prancing around the streets of Washington like Father Christmas?

You see, we arms manufacturers have become one of the most powerful forces in the USA today – as President Eisenhower foresaw. 'We must guard against the acquisition of unwarranted influence . . . by the military–industrial complex,' he said in his farewell address. 'The potential for the disastrous rise of misplaced power exists and will persist.' That was back in 1961, when US military spending was under $47 billion. Now it's more like $282 billion, and everybody is blaming the stock market crash on it.

That, presumably, is why Mr Reagan is suddenly so keen to be seen in public with his arms round a bald man with a birthmark, announcing arms reductions. But merely scrapping 800 missiles isn't going to save the falling dollar, and as a member of the military–industrial complex, I'm certainly not going to stop what I'm doing until somebody tells me what else I can make in my potting-shed.

16 December 1987

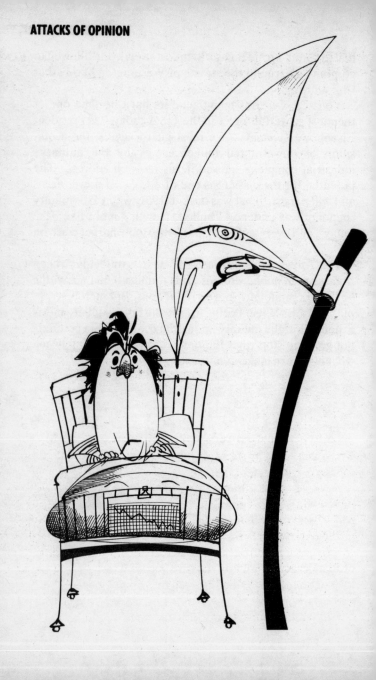

DEMOCRACY

The government really got me thinking last week, when it suddenly found an extra £88 million for the National Health Service and then denied that it was responding to pressure from consultants, surgeons, doctors, nurses, MPs and (according to a Marplan poll) 90 per cent of the British public.

It occurred to me that the whole aim of a democracy is to have a government that is responsive to the wishes of the people. So it seems odd that Mrs Thatcher should make a virtue out of the opposite.

NHS gags doctor critic

ANNABEL FERRIMAN
Health Correspondent

A SENIOR doctor has been suspended from duty and faces disciplinary action for speaking to the Press about her fears regarding cuts in family planning services.

Dr Gillian Cardy, a 50-year-old

And yet maybe she has a point. After all, is the purpose of democracy merely to give the majority of people what they demand? Is something right, simply because the majority want it?

What if the majority of people wanted to put all men,

women and children who have Jewish forebears into little camps with special chambers which can be filled with gas, so that the men, women and children with Jewish forebears die? Would that be right?

Or what if the majority of people agreed it would be a good idea to throw anyone who believes in Christianity into a huge ring with a few starving lions, while everyone who does not believe in Christianity sits around and watches what happens? Would that be right?

Yet history shows us that it is possible to persuade people to go along with such ideas. And – given the persuasive power of TV, radio and the *Sun* – I suppose it would be even easier nowadays. So perhaps an equally important part of democracy lies in providing people with the information on which to base their judgements.

Surgeon accuses Tories of NHS cash deceit

Way back in 1820, Thomas Jefferson (the guy who drafted the American Declaration of Independence) said: 'I know of no safe depository of the ultimate powers of society but the people themselves; and if we think them not enlightened enough to exercise their control with wholesome discretion, the remedy is not to take it from them, but to inform their discretion by education.' Now clearly, Mrs Thatcher is of the opinion that a British public whose 'discretion is informed' by a press owned by Rupert Murdoch, a BBC dictated to by Norman Tebbit and a school curriculum set by Kenneth Baker is simply not worth listening to. And who can blame her?

But what does she do about it? Does she try to provide the public with more information? No – she does her level best to give them even less. Which brings me back to the government's handling of the NHS dispute and its implications for our democracy.

We find the Department of Health trying to suppress reports that reveal the true state of our hospitals. Its civil servants are banned from talking to the press. Staff at Tower Hamlets are 'not permitted to make contacts . . . with Members of Parliament, newspapers, local councillors and health authority members'.

We find a member of the Cabinet declaring it 'intolerable that employees of the health service should openly criticize their health authorities'. And when the President of the Royal College of Surgeons and the President of the British Medical Association sign a petition calling on Mrs Thatcher to increase NHS spending, Conservative central office gets on the phone and persuades them to claim that they didn't.

Bless me! Department of Health experts are now even being told they are covered by the Official Secrets Act!

Thou shalt not talk about the cuts in the NHS in public. Thou shalt not talk about the security services on TV. Thou shalt not talk about politics in school.

This, quite simply, isn't my idea of a democracy . . . and it certainly wasn't Thomas Jefferson's.

23 December 1987

Hospitals forced to reject acute patients

THE POLL TAX

I'd like to say a word in favour of the government's proposal to replace what we call 'the rates' with a 'community charge', or poll tax.

The idea is simple. Since Queen Elizabeth I's time, things like swimming pools, buses, museums, parks and consumer protection have all been provided for by local authorities, elected by people in the area. These local authorities have also been responsible for educating our children, burying our dead, fighting our fires, collecting our rubbish and remunerating our policemen.

To pay for all these so-called services, money has been extorted from the public according to how big their house is. Such a system is blatantly unfair. It takes no account of the fact that, for instance, those with the largest houses have probably got their own swimming pools, and yet they are expected to fork out more than anyone else to pay for public ones. The same with buses. Why on earth should someone who owns, say, two Jaguars and a Mini be forced to shell out vast amounts of loot to subsidize a bus service that they wouldn't be seen dead using?

It is to eradicate injustices like this that the government has decided to bring in the poll tax. This tax simply takes the same amount of money from everybody – regardless of whether they live in a £500,000 house on a private estate in

PEOPLE'S PETITION
AGAINST THE POLL TAX

"We are opposed to the Poll Tax. We believe that it is unfair, unjust and undemocratic. We think the Government should think again."

NAME	ADDRESS

Heseltine heads assault on 'expensive' poll tax

Poll tax hits the festive cheer

Scots count immense cost of launching the poll tax

...ng **organisations include:**
...ay Unit ● British Youth Council ● London Churches Group ● CHAR (Campaign for Single Homeless
...ousing Aid Centre) ● Local Government Information Unit ● NCCL ● Gingerbread ● Church Action on Poverty
...sability Alliance ● British Council of Churches ● London Voluntary Services Council
...eturned to People's Petition c/o 88 Old Street, London EC1V 9HU by 1st June 1988

Printed by Spider Web, 14-16 Sussex Way, London N7

Dulwich or in one room in a council flat off the Peckham Road.

The main thing to remember is that the rates are a tax on property, which is sacred to this government, whereas the poll tax is a tax on human life, which isn't.

After all, when you're in the business of government, you can't afford to be too squeamish about every little fatality that occurs as a result of your policies. What would have happened, for example, if the government had stopped to worry about how many Argies would be drowned when they sank the *Belgrano*? Or what about the Underground system? The government imposed a duty on London Regional Transport to cut cleaning costs and reduce staff, and we really cannot expect it to abandon such ideals merely because a few people get burnt alive.

New charge would be levied on 37 million people

The same goes for unemployment. A recent analysis of the government's own statistics has shown that nowadays 3,000 people are dying every year, because of the strains and stress of being unemployed. And yet what government in its right mind would jeopardize its economic theories for the sake of a few thousand social parasites who can't even earn their own living? Far better to let them go to the wall, and put their dole money to some useful purpose (such as reducing income tax for company directors).

Heavens above! New babies are born every day! People are renewing themselves all the time – in fact, rather too frequently in my opinion. But once a company has gone bankrupt – that's it! No more profits, no more losses, no more anything . . .

Free hand-outs from the state only encourage irresponsibility in people. The poll tax epitomizes the government's determination to bring about a more accountable world, in which everyone pays directly for everything – for their transport, for their housing, for their education, for their water, for their health and now for the very act of being alive. For that, as I said, is the beauty of the new tax: it is a tax on the fact that we exist. It is a tax on life.

30 December 1987

THIRTY YEARS ON

I seem to remember all through the sixties and seventies people becoming increasingly alarmed by the huge increase in deaths from cancers. Cancer was dubbed the Modern Plague, and the medical profession was just as baffled by what was causing it as their medieval counterparts had been by the Black Death.

Back in the fourteenth century one of the favourite theories was that the Plague was caused by a poisonous cloud that had swept over the earth from China. In the sixties and seventies nobody was looking at 'poisonous clouds', but practically every other aspect of modern life fell under suspicion and was investigated.

The one factor which was entirely new in human experience, and whose cancer-forming properties were only just beginning to be recognized, was exposure to certain forms of atomic radiation.

Until recently our estimates of how much radiation human beings can be exposed to had been based on the data provided by the Hiroshima and Nagasaki experiments. However, it is now clear that these estimates grossly underrated the problem, and that, in fact, no level of exposure to radiation is safe – especially since some human beings appear to be more susceptible than others.

The so-called 'safe levels' recommended by such bodies as the National Radiological Protection Board are not actually 'safe levels' at all, but just rough guesses as to how many people will die as a result of a given level of radiation, and what number of such deaths can be considered socially acceptable (by the NRPB), given the enormous benefits of nuclear power and the increasing importance of nuclear reactors as tourist attractions.

Cover-up of fire at Windscale monstrous, charges Tory MP

attributed to serious defects in the Atomic   UK which regulates the tion of our nuclear and establishm

Last week marked the thirtieth anniversary of the 1957 Windscale disaster, when a major fire in the reactor sent a radioactive cloud drifting – not out to sea, as the Atomic Energy Authority claimed at the time – but south-east across most of England. To celebrate the event, the Public Records Office released some (not all) of the top-secret documents that reveal just how bad the disaster was, and just how far those running the country and the industry were prepared to lie in their teeth about it. Far from being a harmless inconvenience, which simply involved throwing a lot of milk down the drain, it now turns out that the 1957 Windscale disaster was far worse than the meltdown at Three Mile Island in 1979, which has since brought the development of nuclear power in the USA to a virtual standstill. Windscale 1957 was more on a par with Chernobyl 1986, and one independent expert (Dr Gofman, Professor Emeritus at the University of California) has estimated that Chernobyl will produce 424,300 cancers in the Soviet Union and 526,700 elsewhere in Europe.

So I wonder how much time and money was wasted in the sixties and seventies, searching for the causes of the Modern Plague, when one very obvious possible cause was, indeed, a poisonous cloud – but one that was brazenly lied out of existence by both the government and the nuclear power industry.

Even last week, I actually heard a spokesman for British Nuclear Fuels Ltd saying on TV: 'Not a single person has ever been killed in a nuclear accident in this country.' It's rather like a spokesman for the motor industry saying that nobody has ever yet been killed on British roads by driving a car . . . Well, it's true! Each year over 5,000 may get killed when their cars hit trees or go under lorries or when they're run over by other people's cars, but no one yet has ever been killed by grasping the steering wheel or by changing gear.

Thousands in UK 'ate lamb contaminated by Chernobyl'

I suppose BNFL is forced to rely on such transparent sophistry because its record is actually the total opposite of what it claims it to be. The nuclear power industry is dangerous, dirty, dear and – as last week's revelations demonstrate beyond all doubt – downright dishonest.

6 January 1988

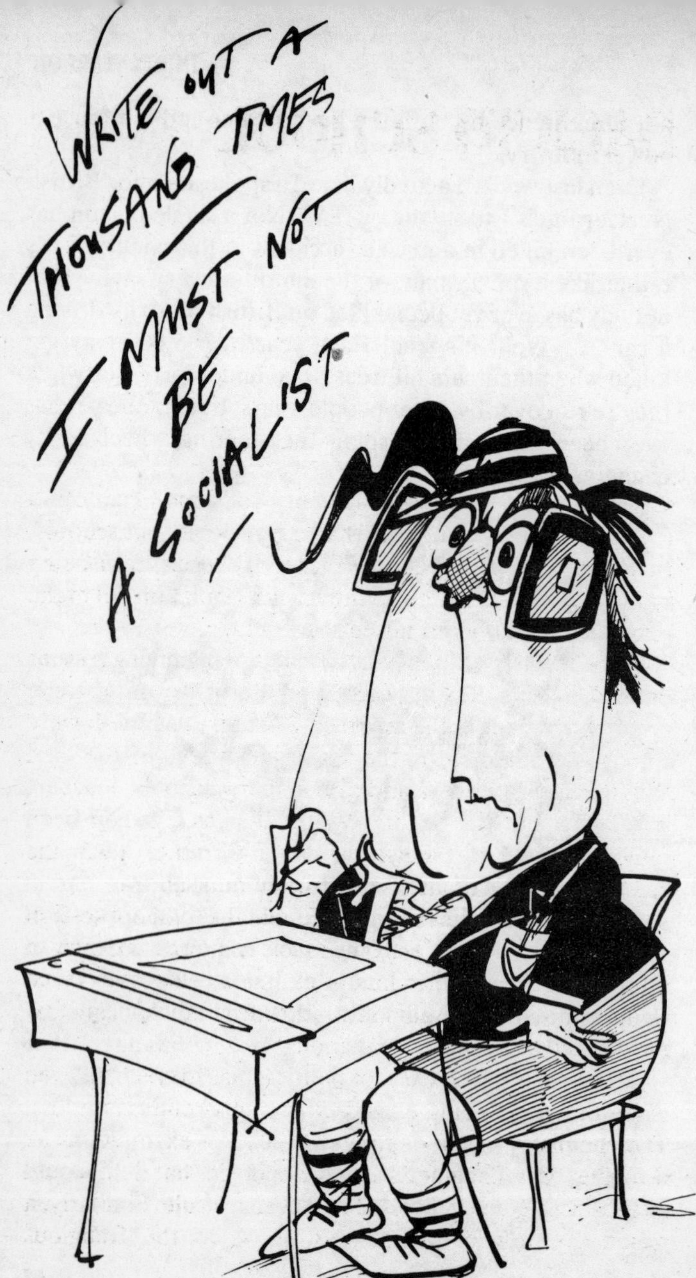
WRITE OUT A THOUSAND TIMES
I MUST NOT BE A SOCIALIST

BACK TO SCHOOL

Well it's the start of a new school term, and once again I find myself worrying about just what is going on in our schools. Is Maggie doing enough to 'protect children from being brain-washed and to keep political indoctrination out of the playground', as she promised she would?

Some teachers, I believe, are still openly giving lessons on the Peasants' Revolt of 1381 and the history of the trade union movement in the nineteenth century as if both were somehow explained by the social conditions of the day! What's more, I understand that in many schools, teachers still talk about the Second World War as if it had been fought against a Fascist dictatorship rather than the creeping menace of international communism!

Of course, all of us are grateful for the 1986 Education Act which, thanks to Baroness Cox and her campaign to take politics out of the classroom, made it illegal to teach partisan political views in schools. But it is now clear that the Act did not go nearly far enough.

You see it is all too easy for political bias to creep in, even when the views being expressed are apparently harmless. The chemistry teacher's tone of voice, for example, as he describes Mrs Thatcher's achievements in that field, could all too easily convey disrespect or even ridicule. Similarly, a raised eyebrow or a sideways smirk, as the Religious

ATTACKS OF OPINION

Instruction teacher spells out the dangers of liberalism in the Church of England, could actually undermine the return to traditional values that the Revd Gummer has demanded.

Once a leftie always a leftie is what I say, and no amount of legislation is going to ensure political balance in such a teacher's classroom.

It seems to me that the only way finally to eradicate politics from the classroom is to vet all teachers for left-wing sympathies. Political activists should be rooted out at the training stage. And though this may mean losing some of the best trainee teachers, extra points could be awarded to the politically apathetic to ensure that enough qualify, and to make up for any intellectual shortcomings or lack of teaching ability in otherwise suitable candidates. Far better to have dull or even uninspiring instructors for our young, than ones with a political axe to grind.

And should any deviants slip through the net, and start sowing the seeds of socialism in our schools, why not encourage pupils to report on any teacher who steps out of line? They could do so anonymously, either to the head-master or else to some regulatory body approved by Conservative central office, and the offender could be booted out before he can guess where his next pay-packet is coming from.

The Prime Minister has declared her ambition to eradicate socialism from these shores by the end of her term in office. So far she and Mr Kinnock have succeeded in eliminating it only from politics. If the good work is going to continue surely it is essential to banish all closet lefties from the classroom (pupils as well as teachers), to suppress all discussion of liberal ideas in schools, and to rid the library shelves once and for all of the works of all subversives like: Karl Marx, Keir Hardie, William Godwin, Robert Owen, William Cobbett, Charles Dickens, H. G. Wells, George Bernard Shaw, Oscar Wilde, Mrs Gaskell, William Blake, Wordsworth, Milton, Burns, Swift, Byron, Shelley and Christ.

13 January 1988

CLAUSE 28

If one person has tender feelings towards another, and wants to promote that other person's happiness, we call this 'love'. Such love is also sometimes accompanied by feelings of sexual attraction.

> Lords defeat for bid to soften gay curb clause

Now if this sort of love occurs between two people whose reproductive arrangements are different, we call it a heterosexual relationship. If the two people have the same reproductive arrangements, we call that a homosexual relationship.

Of course, promoting 'love' of any kind has always been regarded with suspicion by politicians, because it is difficult to make capital out of it. It is much easier to use hatred of the Russians to raise billions of pounds to make weapons than it is to use love of our fellow-men to raise a few quid for the starving in Ethiopia.

So, traditionally, politicians have preferred to court popularity by promoting hatred among their fellow-men – especially hatred of specific minorities, such as school-teachers, social workers, coalminers, Argentinians, Jews or queers. This is the basic philosophy behind Clause 28 of the Local Government Bill, which reaches its committee stage in the House of Lords next Monday.

Clause 28 says: 'A local authority shall not (a) promote homosexuality or . . . (b) promote the teaching in any maintained school of the acceptability of homosexuality as a pretended family relationship.' The Bill seeks to isolate a minority of the population (which has been estimated to be between 10 and 18 per cent of all males) and to discourage the majority from trying to understand or accept them. In other words, in the time-honoured tradition of politicians, it promotes hatred.

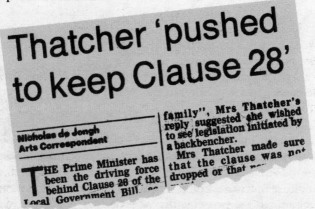

Thatcher 'pushed to keep Clause 28'

Nicholas de Jongh
Arts Correspondent

THE Prime Minister has been the driving force behind Clause 28 of the Local Government Bill, as

family'', Mrs Thatcher's reply suggested she wished to see legislation initiated by a backbencher.

Mrs Thatcher made sure that the clause was not dropped or that

The Bill will mean that if a teacher has a pupil who comes from a loving, caring home, but one in which both parents have the same reproductive arrangements, that teacher will be required by law to teach that child to be ashamed of itself and its home. It will also require all teachers to teach perhaps 10 per cent of the pupils in their classes to regard themselves as unacceptable in society.

Now, of course, I'm as enthusiastic as the next man that the state should compel teachers to lie and to spread hatred and dissension among their pupils, but I can't help feeling that this Bill is actually aimed at the wrong target.

After all, there is no evidence that people who feel attracted to others with the same reproductive arrangements are, as a group, worse citizens, or that they lie and cheat and scheme more than other people. There is, on the other hand, only too much evidence that politicians, as a group, lie and cheat and scheme every day as a matter of course.

Nor do they contribute to our society in other ways. How many politicians are also famous as artists, composers, writers, poets, sculptors, film-makers or thinkers? When you compare politicians and homosexuals, there is absolutely no doubt that homosexuals do far less harm and contribute vastly more to the life of our society.

I would suggest, therefore, that what should be banned in schools is the promotion of politicians as acceptable members of society.

If politicians are allowed to flaunt their way of life, and to make love as freely as they clearly do, both with each other and with innocent members of the public, they will continue to perpetuate their vices.

It is true that some politicians already do have pretended family relationships, but the unfortunate offspring of such pretended relationships cannot be allowed to imagine that there is anything natural about the way their parents behave. It is essential that we do not encourage our children to think that being a politician is in any way compatible with normal, decent, family life.

20 January 1988

THE NHS

In some of the most
recent attacks on the
national health service,
five health centres have
been completely flattened
by mortar fire and one hospital has been dynamited out
of existence. Some thirty-five ambulances have been
ambushed and destroyed, and medical supply vehicles have
been attacked with bazookas. Twenty-one health workers
have been murdered, forty-four have been kidnapped and
four hundred and thirty-one have had all their possessions
destroyed or stolen.

Now, it may come as a surprise to hear that these attacks
were not carried out by the present government against the
health service in Britain, but by the South African-backed
rebels in Mozambique.

Mozambique blames Pretoria for destroying health service

However, I certainly think that our Prime Minister could
learn a thing or two from her colleagues in the Mozambique

National Resistance. Their techniques have achieved results in a short space of time far beyond Mrs Thatcher's wildest dreams.

They have managed to close down 31 per cent of the country's health centres and increased deaths among children under five to 325–75 in every 1,000. Not bad going for a bunch of guerillas with no mandate from the people, no tame TV or press, and not even a John Moore to do their dirty work.

In 1986 alone, the Mozambique rebels were able to kill some 84,000 children by disrupting the national health care programme. This is far better than anything the British government has been able to achieve in this field. Here, child-deaths caused by government health policies can be numbered only in hundreds rather than thousands.

Private bed plan as heart boy dies

Take Birmingham, for example, one of the largest conurbations in the country, and yet there are only some 600 children whose heart operations are being held up by nursing shortages. And even then not all of these kids can be certain to die. If the parents make enough fuss, and manage to get questions asked in the House of Commons, the Prime Minister will inevitably be forced to make a concession and allow their child its operation. It is true that the child's condition will have deteriorated considerably in the meantime, but that's not quite the same thing as death.

The point is that the whole process seems very cack-handed compared to the direct approach of the Mozambique National Resistance.

As for closing down hospitals, I can't understand why the British government persists in footling around running hospitals down piecemeal, by starving them of resources, funds and nurses, when they could follow the lead of the MNR and simply blow them up! That would be quicker, simpler and far cheaper. It would also relieve the NHS of one of the most costly elements in all health care – patients.

At the moment, the government's only method of reducing the back-log of unwanted patients is the rather serendipitous one of leaving them on waiting-lists for several years, in the hope that they will, in the meantime, die of their own volition. But this works only with the elderly or with acute cases. Far too many are still slipping through and getting into hospital beds at the taxpayers' expense.

GPs say they are Thatcher's next target

Of course, it must be said that the aims of the British government and the rebels in Mozambique in attacking their respective health services are not identical. The MNR are trying (with South Africa's help) to destabilize their government, whereas nothing could be further from the mind of the British Prime Minister. Her aim is simply to undermine the system of free, unquestioned medical treatment for all, regardless of wealth, and to make more people pay for being sick.

If Mrs Thatcher is ever to restore health as a commodity to be bought and sold, she must stop pussy-footing around, and tackle the problem head-on, like they are in Mozambique.

27 January 1988

BRITISH JUSTICE

British Justice can't (and doesn't) always get the right verdict, as poor old Timothy Evans could tell us, if he hadn't been hanged by his neck until he was dead for a murder he didn't commit.

British Justice is interpreted by human beings, and all human beings are fallible. It would not be reasonable to expect 100 per cent accuracy of British Justice – or of anyone else's justice. But then I was always taught that British Justice is not revered throughout the world because it gets it right every time, but because it is impartial and keeps itself beyond the influence of politicians.

Recently, however, there has been a concerted effort to expand and improve British Justice, by getting it to look beyond the petty, everyday questions of guilt or innocence, right or wrong, and to focus on the wider context.

Increasingly, some of our most eminent guardians of the law are voicing the opinion that a little crime here and there is perfectly all right – it just depends on who is committing it and against whom. For example, Lord Donaldson, who is the present Master of the Rolls (at a salary of £74,750 per year and a clean criminal record), has recently said in public that it's all right to break the law if you happen to be a member of MI5. In fact, he said that our security services could hardly get by without a bit of burglary from time to

THE SUN SAYS

Real justice

A BLACK day for justice. A case will haunt judges and politicians.

Can those words really h... been spoken by a **BRITISH** about the Appeal Court's ver... on the Birmingham Six?

To the eternal shame of Chris Mullin, Labour MP for Su... derland South, that was h... venomous verdict.

His outburst would have do... *credit to a Falls Road Fenia...*

The facts are simple: ... men accused of

Loony MP backs the IRA pub bombing monsters

Bomb trial 'biased by link to IRA'

The six Irishmen gaoled for life for the Birmingham pub ... suffered considerable ... because they stood ... three men who had ... Court ...

Long fight to free men in vain

Relatives pledge to continue their struggle

AFTER the decision was announced, Mr Patrick ... shall not stop. We shall be ... intensifying time. (I expect he's been watching a lot of James Bond films.)

Then, only last week, the Director of Public Prosecutions for Northern Ireland and Sir Patrick Mayhew, the Attorney-General (both, incidentally, with spotless criminal records), agreed that no one should be prosecuted for attempting to pervert the course of justice or for murdering certain members of the public in Northern Ireland – not because these things hadn't happened, but because putting them in the spotlight of British Justice would 'not be in the public interest'. That is to say: it might open up a can of worms, revealing a vast conspiracy to cover up a policy of murder by the Royal Ulster Constabulary.

This echoes something said, back in 1980, by Lord Denning (who was then Master of the Rolls and of equally good character). He declared that British Justice should not try to find out whether or not the police had beaten confessions out of the Birmingham Bomber Monsters – not because they clearly hadn't, but because if they had it would open up 'such an appalling vista' of perjury, violence and intimidation by the British police and would so embarrass the Home Secretary 'that every sensible person in the land would say that it cannot be right these actions should go any further'.

It is in this context that we should view the decision of the three Appeal Court Lords not to order a retrial of the Birmingham Bomber Monsters (I use the words of our leading legal journal, the *Sun*). Whether the six are guilty or not guilty is clearly irrelevant, because, according to the testimony of Lord Denning, Lord Donaldson, Sir Patrick Mayhew and the Director of Public Prosecutions for Northern Ireland, guilt or innocence is no longer the overriding objective of British Justice. Nowadays, British Justice's chief concern must be 'the public good' and 'the national interest'.

ATTACKS OF OPINION

If the Birmingham Bomber Monsters should ever turn out not to be the Birmingham Bomber Monsters after all, 'the public good' and 'the national interest' (as defined by those in a position to define them) would be dealt a series of grave blows. We would have to face up to: corruption in the police force, incompetence in our Home Office forensic service and either gullibility or partiality in our judiciary . . . Heavens above! We might even be forced to review the cases of the Maguire Seven Bomber Monsters and the Guildford Four Bomber Monsters, about all of whose convictions doubts persist.

And so, British Justice strides boldly forwards towards the end of the twentieth century and towards its new and wider role in our society, steered by some of the greatest legal intellects of our age.

Oh brave new world that has such people in it . . .

3 February 1988

TOO MUCH FOOD

We Europeans have a big problem on our plates – literally. You see, our modern farming methods have become so successful that we are now producing far more food than we can actually eat.

Storing the stuff is no solution because that costs money. Besides, most governments would prefer to store something exciting like radioactive waste or dioxin.

Charles calls for action on pollution

THE Prince of Wales yesterday challenged the Government and called for action to protect the North Sea from further pollution.

If science ha anything.

And obviously we can't just give the stuff away to the Sudanese or the Ethiopians or anybody who actually needs it, because that would be too simple.

So the only solution is to produce less.

You might think that after millions of years of trying to produce enough, nothing could be easier than to try and produce less. But it is actually a rather tricky problem.

The British government has come up with the brilliant wheeze of simply giving every farmer a prize of £200 per hectare of farmland that he can let go to waste or persuade someone to build a bingo hall on.

Now, the reason our farmers have become so efficient at producing more food than we need is because of the Wonders of Modern Science – otherwise known as 'intensive farming techniques'. Unlike our ignorant forefathers, farmers nowadays heap artificial fertilizers and pesticides on the land and these have become major pollutants. The artificial fertilizers, for example, get washed through the

Minister agrees clean-up for nitrate-ridden water

soil and contaminate our drinking water with nitrate. This, according to the World Health Organization, can lead to methaemoglobinaemia (which admittedly kills only smaller babies). What's more, nitrite (as nitrate becomes once you've eaten it) may also possibly lead to stomach cancer in adults. Meanwhile, the pesticides kill off our wildlife, pollute our seas and rivers and, of course, get left as residues in the fruit and vegetables we eat.

So you might imagine that a more sensible way of cutting back on farm production would be to encourage farmers to use less artificial fertilizer and pesticide, and to go back to the older methods of farming. But again that would be far too simple.

You see, manufacturing fertilizers and pesticides is really big business for companies like ICI and Norsk-Hydro. We now spend something like £450 million a year on fertilizers and about £350 million a year on pesticides, and you can't stop a bandwagon like that just because it's contaminating our drinking water or poisoning our children and wildlife.

So this is where we come to the beauty of the government's scheme. If farmers reduce their farmland, they will, inevitably, try to keep up the same level of production (and income) by growing more on what they've got left. In other words, they will farm even more intensively, and use even more artificial fertilizers and pesticides than they did before! This, of course, will be great news for ICI and Norsk-Hydro, but not such good news, perhaps, for people who still drink tap-water in parts of East Anglia, Lincolnshire, Nottinghamshire and Staffordshire, where nitrate contamination of the water supply already exceeds the WHO's recommended limits.

It is true that, as a sop to these people (and because it's been acting illegally up to now), the government has promised to denitrify their water, even though this will cost the taxpayer hundreds of millions of pounds and will lead to other problems. The main thing is that at least it won't cut into the profits of ICI and Norsk-Hydro – and the profits of big business are, after all, the one thing that most governments nowadays seem to be really good at protecting.

10 February 1988

IGNORANCE

Hermon faces possible disciplinary case

I was relieved to read that the Chief Constable of the Royal Ulster Constabulary, Sir John Hermon, has claimed that he didn't know that officers under his command had concocted a cover up and had lied to the Northern Irish Director of Public Prosecutions over the alleged shoot to kill business.

As everyone knows, Ignorance is the best defence one can offer in public life. It used not to be, but it is now.

Attorney-General refuses to publish report of inquiry

Stalker found no formal RUC 'shoot to kill' policy

President Reagan, for example, was ignorant of the fact that the proceeds from the illegal sales of arms to Iran were going to fund his favourite charity – the Contras. (The Contras, you remember, are those Nicaraguans dedicated to bringing down their democratically elected government by murdering its supporters.)

Mrs Thatcher was ignorant of the peace plan that the Argentinians were on the verge of accepting when she sank the *Belgrano*, and made it impossible for the Argies to accept anything. At the time, of course, Mrs Thatcher's popularity rating was the lowest of any Prime Minister's since such polls began, and it's well known that there is no better fillip for a PM's ratings than a little, self-contained war on foreign soil. So without the plea of Ignorance, Mrs Thatcher might have been suspected of sending the *Belgrano* to the bottom (with the loss of 368 lives) simply to ensure that she wasn't cheated of her war.

Mrs Thatcher was also ignorant about the leaking of the Solicitor-General's letter to Michael Heseltine during the Westland Affair. This, you may remember, was another very fortunate piece of Ignorance, because Mr Heseltine had had the effrontery to oppose her wishes, and the Solicitor-General's letter conveniently discredited him.

> Mayhew cites national security on 'shoot to kill'
>
> # Officers escape prosecution in Stalker case

In all these cases, Ignorance was accepted as a perfectly respectable defence. There was a time, however, when, if a person in a position of power admitted Ignorance about what was being done in his name, he would think it his duty to offer his resignation, on the grounds that if he didn't know what his subordinates were doing, he jolly well ought to. We are, indeed, fortunate that modern attitudes are so much more enlightened.

But don't imagine the plea of Ignorance works for everyone all the time. It doesn't usually work, for instance, for the schoolboy who is caught with twenty Rothmans in his pocket. Nor does it often work for the small-time crook. 'I did not know I had thirty-nine stolen video recorders in the back of my van, Your Honour' is usually a losing line in court. It certainly didn't work for Captain Heywood, when he told the Swedes that he didn't know the car he was driving was full of drugs.

So how and when can you legitimately use the plea of Ignorance?

It seems to work better the more important you are and the more you could be expected to know what is going on. Thus it is best employed by heads of state with access to any amount of information that is unavailable to the general public. Presidents, Prime Ministers and so on, with spies and secret service reports and all the information-gathering techniques of a modern state at their fingertips, can plead Ignorance with total confidence.

The main thing to bear in mind is that the more unlikely it is, the more the defence of Ignorance tends to carry weight.

For myself, I'm thinking of using it next time I'm had up on a mugging charge, but I have a feeling it won't wash. I suppose I might have more chance if I were to tell them I'm Sir John Hermon, but even then . . .

24 February 1988

UNDERGROUND

Last week, London Regional Transport invited travellers to write and tell them how to improve the Tube system. Here's my letter.

Dear LRT,

It's four years now since Mrs T. told wicked old London Transport to get stuffed, and put in you boys to slim down the Underground system into a profit-making business that she could sell off. And you've been doing a terrific job.

You've got rid of no less than 1,688 of your staff in the last three years! That's some achievement.

Of course, the Underground is now filthier, less reliable and more dangerous than it's ever been, but that isn't really your concern. Your job is to get it to make a profit, and I know you'll do it.

You've already cut the budget for lift and escalator maintenance from £11 million to £6 million. And booting out all those cleaners must have really saved a packet. At King's Cross, for example, I believe you reduced the cleaning staff from fourteen to two and a part-timer. And I understand that the escalators are now cleaned only once a week instead of every night. Well done!

Stupidity blamed for deaths in Tube fire

Litter was not the Tube culprit

TERRY JONES (Young Guardian, March 2) is entitled to his little joke, but the evidence on which he bases his views is faulty. A great deal of nonsense has been written about the Underground since the King's Cross fire and Mr Jones appears to have accepted the mythology as fact.

Take for example the oft-repeated claim that cleaning staff at King's Cross had been "reduced from 14 to two and a part-timer." In fact, the number of cleaners was increased from zero to about eight (two full-time day, one part-time evening, and a heavy overnight gang of up to six). At the same time the lowest grade of station staff whose duties previously included some cleaning was reduced from 16 (not 14) to 10.

The remarks about litter causing fires and that saving lives "isn't your business" are at best offensive but this whole line of argument implies that King's Cross was a litter fire; it was not. It began in the layer of lubricating grease under the chain drive of the escalator.

There were no changes made in cleaning methods affecting this part of the machinery in recent years and no cleaning regime would alter the fact that even the small amount of grease essential for the operation of the machine will burn. We have been studying the use of fire resistant lubricants, but many have sometimes overriding disadvantages.

The main theme of Mr Jones's article was that making money is our sole objective. A requirement to reduce costs was only one of the objectives set by the Government in 1984.
Tony M. Ridley.
Chairman,
London Underground.

A cleaner count that was not so wide of the mark

TONY RIDLEY, the chairman of London Underground, takes me to task (Letters, March 7) for suggesting that the cleaning staff at King's Cross has been reduced from 14 to two and a part-timer. In fact, he claims, the number of cleaners has actually increased from "zero to about eight."

Of course, by "zero" Mr Ridley doesn't actually mean that previously there weren't any people cleaning the station — it's just that they weren't called "cleaners." They were, in fact, called "railmen," and — surprise! surprise! — there were 14 of them. These "railmen" have now been phased out completely.

In their place, London Underground has started to employ "cleaners." Mr Ridley lists these as: "two full-time day, one part-time evening, and a heavy overnight gang of up to six." The thing he omits to say is that this "heavy overnight gang" is not actually based at King's Cross, but just cleans it as and when it can among other stations. It should not therefore be counted in as part of the full-time King's Cross cleaning staff.

Take them away and lo and behold! you are left with two full-time and one part-time. So it seems that the "oft-repeated claim" that the cleaning staff at King's Cross has been reduced from 14 to two and a part-timer isn't that wide of the mark after all — provided you know about "cleaners" and "railmen."
Terry Jones
London NW1.

You weren't to know that litter could cause fires (even though it happened at Bradford City Football Club and the fire brigade warned you it could happen in the Tube). Saving lives isn't your business. Your business is saving money, and that's what you did. What's more, I know we can rely on you to keep rebuilding costs (and victim compensation) down to a minimum.

But what to do about the litter? Obviously the last thing you want to do is to go back to employing more cleaners, so I would suggest you stop passengers taking anything that could become litter into the Tube system. Handbags and pockets should be searched at the ticket barrier, and any droppable articles (such as wrapping-paper, tickets, banknotes) should be either confiscated or securely tied on to the prospective traveller with lengths of string.

There should also be really tough prison sentences for anyone caught smoking on the Tube and for children who eat sweets or ice-creams while travelling.

It might also be a good idea to issue every passenger with a brush or duster. I see no excuse for travellers to loll around in idleness while waiting for trains. It's high time they were put to work cleaning up the place.

Now I know a lot of wiseacres are saying that it's the cuts in staffing levels that have caused most of the problems since you took over – there are more muggings, less information, dirtier trains and no one to help out in an emergency like King's Cross. But it's also quite obvious that cutting staff is the only way to make the Underground pay, and I know you've got the ultimate objective of abolishing staff altogether at some stations. So my suggestion is: why not go the whole hog and abolish passengers as well?

Without passengers, there would be no need to install expensive automatic barriers and ticket machines. Cleaning staff could probably be cut down to a couple of elderly ladies with mops for the entire system. There would be no need to heat or light the stations, and the frequency of trains could be dramatically reduced down to one or two a day – or even none! The stations and tunnels could then be sold off either as nuclear-proof office accommodation or else for growing mushrooms.

It's time that people began to understand that the Underground isn't simply there for their convenience – it's there to make money. That is the only objective Mrs T. has set you, and that's what you must do, regardless of what or who has to suffer in the process.

2 March 1988

MAKING POVERTY PAY

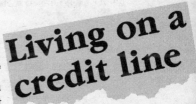

Last week's report from the Child Poverty Action Group* records an incident in which a young girl was refused a grant for shoes. The Department of Health and Social Security official who turned down her application advised her parents that, since they had already admitted that the girl possessed no less than three pairs of socks, she should wear all three together, and that would make a suitable alternative to shoes.

I trust the official in question has already received an Award For Ingenuity in Saving Taxpayers' Money from Mrs Thatcher. He deserves it.

However, while applauding the spirit of this particular solution, I do feel there are even more ways in which creative DHSS officials can reduce the costs of sponging off the state. Here are a few modest proposals of my own.

Poor parents who apply for grants to heat their homes could have their smaller children removed from them and packed into boxes. These boxes could then be placed under the desks of DHSS officials. The warmth generated by the

* *Single Payments: The Disappearing Safety Net* is available, price £3.98 (including postage), from the Child Poverty Action Group Ltd, 1–5 Bath Street, London EC1V 9PY.

combined bodies in the boxes would serve to keep the DHSS officials warm and save the Department millions of pounds in heating bills.

Shake-up in benefit hits elderly first

Suicide after DHSS's letter

I might add that such a solution would probably come as a blessing to a lot of parents in those many areas of the country where there is no longer any nursery care available.

Another timely idea might be for all old people (no matter what they are claiming) to donate their teeth to the Department. Teeth are surprisingly heavy and, if sewn into little bags, would make excellent paperweights. These would be invaluable in keeping the millions of pending applications in their place. Teeth-bags could also be used as doorstops, to keep the DHSS doors permanently open, so that unsuccessful claimants could pass in and out more rapidly and in larger numbers.

Poor families, who have nothing to sleep on and who apply for bedding grants, could be stripped and shaved. The hair thus collected (once it has been properly sterilized and debugged) could be used to stuff the seats of DHSS officials – thus easing the many tedious hours they have to sit and listen to the whingeing and whining of the lowest members of society. Furthermore, the bedding applications could then be turned down on the grounds that the applicants look odd without any hair.

As for unmarried women who have the effrontery to beg for money with which to feed their offspring, they should be harangued for several hours in public about the immorality of their situation, and then sold off to the white slave trade (which, I believe, still flourishes in some more enlightened parts of the world). Their surviving offspring could be put in the boxes which I mentioned previously.

Single mother suffers weekly loss of £45

In ways like these, I am convinced, it might soon be possible to turn the Department of Health and Social Security around from a constant drain on the taxpayers' pockets into a profit-making concern. And that, as I understand it, is the ultimate goal of everything that concerns this government.

Certainly it cannot be denied that, with a profitable DHSS, Mr Lawson (who you may remember as the Chancellor of the Exchequer) would have considerably more than a mere £4 billion to give away to those who really need it – such as three-car families in Weybridge.

9 March 1988

TRUE CONFESSIONS

I've always wondered why people will persist in confessing to crimes that they haven't committed, and the recent case of David Blythe really had me puzzled.

When Mr Blythe was eighteen, he was arrested for the murder of two elderly sisters in the Manchester area. He confessed to the murders, and then, some time later, it turned out that somebody totally different had done them.

Now, since we know that British policemen don't beat confessions out of prisoners, I'd like to know what motivates any man to confess to something that he knows he hasn't done – particularly a double murder?

Off-duty policemen in pub beating claim

I suppose a lot of cases may happen when a suspect is so bored with hour after hour of polite questions from friendly cheerful policemen that he caves in – especially when (as in Mr Blythe's case) there is not even a lawyer present to relieve the monotony of ceaseless good humour and respectful inquiry.

POLICEMAN: And so, Mr Suspect, sir, you are absolutely totally a hundred per cent completely and honestly positive, sir, that it was not you what done this ghastly double murder in which two sweet old ladies aged ninety-two and eighty-one were savagely beaten to death, blood on the walls and so on?

SUSPECT: For the four thousandth time *no*! Oh, all right – *yes*!

POLICEMAN: Gotcha!

Woman officer beat me up – ex-policeman

A VICIOUS and unprovoked assault by a police officer on an innocent man is too petty to go to court, the Director of Public Prosecutions has ruled.

Now the victim, Mr Owen Gape, aged 58, who was a police officer for 26 years, says : 'I'll never trust a copper again.'

get out of the ------- car, you'll get out of the ------- car.''

Mr Gape asked the PC to call a senior officer. But he claims the officer replied : 'We don't need any senior officer, mate.'

Mr Gape said : 'All the time the WPC was continually shout-

or lift a finger. If I had done so, any injuries i received would have been claimed as caused by resisting arrest and I would have been charged with assaulting them.'

Another possibility is that they confess by mistake. After all, there is only a single word of difference between: 'I most certainly did *not* do the ghastly crime with blood spattered on the walls and so on' and 'I most certainly *did* do the ghastly crime with blood spattered on the walls and so on.'

It would be quite understandable if, under the complete lack of pressure of a police interrogation, and in the friendly relaxed atmosphere of an interview room when no lawyer is present, that a little word here and there might get forgotten. And 'not' is a particularly tiny and insignificant word anyway – especially when you're on such an important charge as murder.

Another possibility, of course (and I am here in no way suggesting any criticism of the police), is that a suspect's original 'confession' gets misheard.

I mean, despite the magnificent record of the police in taking down literally millions of statements over the years, and getting each and every literary nuance just right every time, it is (I suppose) just conceivable that certain special circumstances could make it difficult for the interrogating officer to hear everything perfectly. There may be, for example, screams and banging and abuse coming from the interrogation room next door, as some friendly constable re-enacts highlights from the previous night's *A-Team* for the entertainment of some slightly bored IRA suspect.

Or it could be that a bit of bacon fat from the staff canteen gets lodged in the interrogating officer's ear, and makes it difficult for him to pick up on little words of less than two syllables. But on the whole, and knowing the police reputation for getting their food into the right orifice, I think that this is highly unlikely.

Perhaps the most probable hypothesis, however, is that well-intentioned suspects in these cases are so anxious not to waste police time, with hours of unnecessary answering, that they simply confess straight off, and then retract later on.

Of course, there is no suggestion of any of these things having happened in Mr Blythe's case – nor, indeed, of anything improper having occurred at all, but false confessions still remain a mystery – as I'm sure the six Birmingham Bomber Monsters would be the first to agree.

16 March 1988

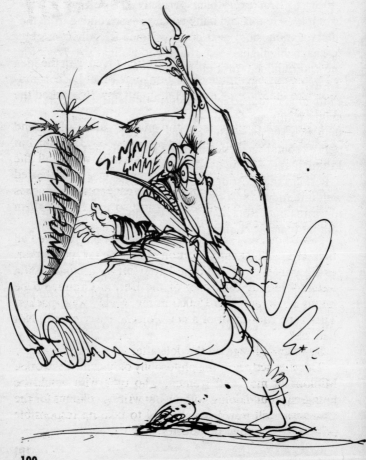

INCENTIVES

Thatcher triumphant

THE Prime Minister yesterday launched a withering assault on her political opponents and pronounced last Tuesday's Budget 'the boldest reforming budgets time'. She went on: for socialism'. the

I don't know about you, but I've often toyed with the idea of becoming Chairman of ICI or some other big corporation like the Burton Group, but up till now I've lacked the motivation.

I know ICI pays their top man a salary of around £300,000 a year, while the Burton job pays £1.3 million, but I've always wondered whether it's really worth all the inconvenience of being driven around in a chauffeured limousine, or the bother of having to eat expensive lunches with ministers and civil servants just so you can tell them what you'd like them to do.

Now, however, Nigel Lawson's budget has changed all that! His brilliant simplification of income tax means that, as Chairman of ICI, I'd be better off by around £900 a week! While as Chairman of the Burton Group, I'd be taking home an extra £5,000 in my weekly wage-packet. That's the equivalent of a new Porsche every month! Not bad, eh?

So I think I'll sign off the dole after all, and go for it.

This is exactly how the philosophy of 'incentives' works. Millions of men and women, who otherwise would be lounging around doing nothing but writing columns for the *Guardian*, will now be motivated to take up responsible positions as captains of industry.

And what of those who are already captains of industry? Well, of course, the extra £247,000 a year that Nigel Lawson has presented to the Chairman of the Hanson Trust, for example, will obviously encourage Lord Hanson to work much harder than he has in the past. While the extra quarter of a million pounds a year he's given to the Burton boss will really make Sir Ralph Halpern knuckle down, roll up his sleeves and put his nose to the grindstone. It is a well-known fact (even though a recent government study failed to prove it was) that government hand-outs on this scale increase the efficiency and productivity of the rich no end.

It's the rich what gets the pleasure . . .

Of course, the same can't be said of the poor, because, as we all know, they are unbelievably greedy, and the more you give them, the more time off they'll want to spend it in. No, with the incorrigibly poor, incentives work the other way round, and the only way to get them up off their backsides is to make life as intolerable and humiliating for them as we possibly can. That was the philosophy behind the Victorian work-house, and it's an idea whose time has clearly come again.

This is why, next month, the government will be reducing the amount available as one-off payments to help poor families buy basic essentials (such as bedding and floor-coverings) from £173 million to £60 million. That's a saving of nearly 5,000 Porsches!

Altogether there will be a total of only £200 million available for emergency payments (£140 million of which poor families will have to pay back with whatever they can beg, borrow or, of course, steal), even though the government's own Social Security Advisory Committee considers £350 million to be the bare minimum needed to avoid hardship and distress. But, of course, hardship and distress are the last things the government wants to avoid, if the poor are to be made to stand on their own two feet. Only hardship and distress will persuade the poor to start trying to sell off their children's clothes or cutting down on the amount they eat, instead of pestering that nice Mr Moore.

So, while Mr Lawson's social fund will claw back £150 million from those on the breadline (enough to provide 720 Rolls-Royce Phantom VI limousines for those who really need them), he'll be dishing out eleven times that amount to the richest 5 per cent of our society. That's the equivalent of 75,578 Maserati Turbo 425s!

And that's why I'm taking over ICI as soon as I bloody well can! It's going to get not just uncomfortable at the bottom of the pile, but positively dangerous, once the government starts to show us what they really mean by 'incentives'.

23 March 1988

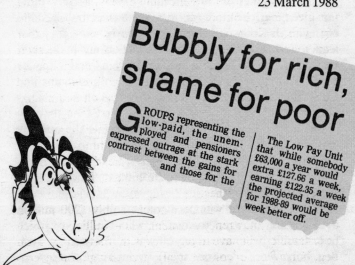

Bubbly for rich, shame for poor

GROUPS representing the low-paid, the unemployed and pensioners expressed outrage at the stark contrast between the gains for and those for the

The Low Pay Unit that while somebody £63,000 a year would extra £127.66 a week, earning £122.35 a week the projected average for 1988-89 would be week better off.

RO-RO-RO'S

Last week a court ruled that it is illegal for the National Union of Seamen to ballot their members about striking.

The obvious danger to society in finding out what people think by allowing them to vote hardly needs to be stressed by someone like myself. And (to do them justice for once) our political leaders have recently become more forthright in expressing their distaste for the process of voting. Mrs Thatcher doesn't like the inhabitants of our big cities voting for their metropolitan councils – so she abolishes the councils. Mr Kinnock doesn't like his party voting for a new leader – so he calls it a 'needless distraction' and looks very, very cross indeed. The late Dr David Owen doesn't like the SDP voting to merge with another party whose name I've forgotten – so he ignores the result. And so on . . .

Last week's ruling, however, is the first time that the courts have brought the whole thing out into the open by making it actually illegal to vote for something. The background is as follows.

P & O Adventure Ferries plc are doing their best to bring back excitement into the sea-faring business. They insist on using the wonderfully unpredictable 'roll-on roll-off roll-over' ferries (known as ro-ro-ro's), whose ability to capsize has already been so successfully demonstrated by such vessels as: *The European Gateway* (which capsized outside

Harwich), *The Herald of Free Enterprise* (which capsized outside Zeebrugge) and, most recently, by *The Vinca Gorthon* (which capsized earlier this month in the North Sea).

The 'roll-on roll-off roll-over' ferries can achieve in a matter of 180 seconds what it takes a conventional ship half an hour to do, i.e. capsize. It's a bit like crossing the Channel on a greasy log.

Seamen go to court to fight for ballot

Naval designers demand tougher ferry safety laws

And now P & O are trying to pack even more thrills into each voyage by keeping their crews on duty for twenty-four hours at a stretch and by reducing their numbers by a third.

Of course, whenever anyone tries to make things more fun, the killjoys start bleating about 'safety' and so on. In this case, first the official inquiry into *The Herald of Free Enterprise* disaster said that 'roll-on roll-off roll-over' ferries should be junked or else modified. Then last week the Royal Institute of Naval Architects, representing 6,600 (I never knew there were so many) ship designers, jumped on to the bandwagon by claiming that 'ro-ro-ro's' are 'unacceptably vulnerable' to capsizing, and that the government ought to ban them as they stand.

ATTACKS OF OPINION

Fortunately, however, the Department of Transport shares P & O's enthusiasm for Adventure at Sea, and has so far refused to pass any legislation to make 'roll-on roll-off roll-overs' any less exciting.

But then the National Union of Seamen decided to stick their oar in. The Union wanted to ballot its members about striking over the reduction in staffing levels and the diminishing safety standards on British merchant ships.

Well, I ask you! What business is it of theirs? Why should men who have put absolutely no investment into the industry (apart from their lives) be permitted to dictate conditions that would substantially reduce the record profits that P & O have only so recently announced?

Mr Justice Michael Davies is to be congratulated on taking the first bold step in clamping down on the excesses of the ballot-box. If we are to curb the absurd powers of popular opinion, and allow management the right to manage as it sees fit, then we are going to need a lot more court rulings like this – no matter who ends up at the bottom of the sea.

31 March 1988

THE END OF POVERTY

Tory ideology 'promoting poverty'

THE Government was accused yesterday of promoting

The government is going to abolish poverty, and I think they're making a big mistake.

Of course, they are not actually going to reduce the number of people who can't afford to feed their children or put shoes on their feet – that would undermine the whole delicate edifice of the Incentive Society, on which so much effort and love have been lavished in the last nine years.

You see, an Incentive Culture depends on some people being incredibly rich and some people being incredibly poor. In fact, the more incredibly poor people there are, the more incentive there is for them to improve themselves and, therefore, for more people to work harder. It's all quite logical really.

So rather than reduce the number of poor people, the government is actually more interested in increasing it. And wonderful progress has already been made.

Between 1979, when Mrs Thatcher seized power (I'm sorry! There I go again using the phraseology our popular newspapers use when a left-wing council gets elected), and 1983 the government managed to increase the number of people living in poverty by 50 per cent. It is reckoned that by now there must be at least 11 million people living on or below the poverty line. That is one in five of the population of this great and affluent country of ours. Some achievement, eh?

And, as if all that weren't enough, the government has also succeeded beyond anyone's wildest dreams in making the incredibly poor incredibly poorer. Of course, pleasant-spoken chaps like Mr John Major 'will be very happy' to tell us that the government is spending more than ever before on what it gives to the poor. But then that's because there are more of them.

In fact, the poor now pay more in taxes than they did in 1979, and receive less in compensation. A low-paid married couple without children, for instance, in 1983 paid 30 per cent more in direct taxes than they did in 1979. While a retired couple will have seen their annual income reduced by £750 a year under Mrs Thatcher.

Poverty group warns of gaping hole in safety net

Of course, while statistics like these are great news for the Incentive Society, they are just the sort of figures that could be used by unscrupulous opponents of the government to sour the minds of the disgruntled and disaffected in our midst. This is why the government wisely delayed the publication of the *Low Income Family Statistics for 1983* until 1986, and – even then – sneaked them into the House of Commons Library at the last possible moment, when most MPs were on their way home for the holidays.

This is also why the government is now to abolish poverty. At least, what they plan to do is to abolish the statistics by which poverty is now estimated.

The DHSS (which is the department in charge of reducing the amount the government is forced to give the poor) plans to replace the *Low Income Family Statistics* with something called *Households Below Average Income: A Statistical Analysis*. These new figures will simply relate low incomes to the average. In other words, according to the Low Pay Unit, they'll just tell us who is doing better than whom, rather than who can and who can't afford to feed their families.

Thatcher tells widow, aged 73, to borrow to make ends meet

Personally, I can't understand why, when Mr Lawson has attained popular stardom through his success in making the rich richer, the government should still be inhibited about publicizing its achievements in making the poor poorer. After all, the growth of poverty is part and parcel of the Incentive Society. So why be coy about it? If you've got it – flaunt it! And poverty should be no exception.

6 April 1988

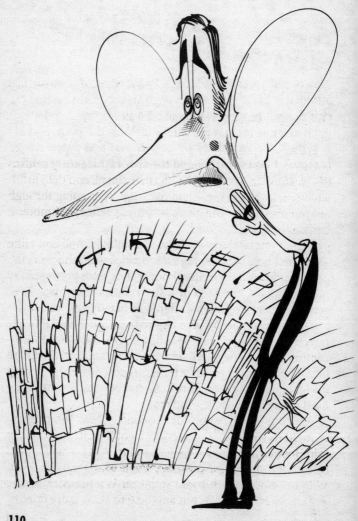

MODERN CITIES

'Why spend Easter in Holland?' I asked.

'You'll like it,' said my wife.

I did.

But as I wandered around the sixteenth-century centres of Amsterdam and Delft, with their canals and delightful, wide-windowed houses, one question kept going through my mind: why are old cities beautiful places and modern cities ugly places?

It can't just be that we all like old buildings and don't like new ones, because when these old cities were still new, the people who built them also thought they were pretty snazzy places. In fact, throughout history, cities and towns have generally been regarded as things of beauty and wonder.

Throughout the Middle Ages they are invariably referred to as 'fair' or 'beautiful'. Go back to fourth-century Rome, and you'll find one poet calling it 'the home of the gods', while another tells us that it possesses 'beauty no imagination can picture'. As for Naples – well! They used to say: 'See Naples and die!'

And the same went for London. Dick Whittington thought its streets were paved with gold, while Dr Johnson told Boswell in no uncertain terms that 'When a man is tired of London, he is tired of life.' Even as recently as 1802, William Wordsworth could stand on Westminster Bridge and declare: 'Earth has not anything to show more fair.'

What has happened between Wordsworth's time and ours?

Why are today's cities things to be escaped from for the weekend? London is 'The Smoke' or 'The Great Wen'. Its tentacles spread so deep into the countryside that now the highest praise an estate agent can heap on a place of natural beauty is to call it 'unspoilt'.

What has gone wrong? Why are old cities like Delft and Amsterdam congenial, habitable arrangements of bricks and mortar, while their modern outskirts are purgatories of anonymity?

If modern science and technology have given us such wonderful capacity to shape and control our environment, why are we apparently incapable of creating cities in which people actually want to live?

I have to tell you: I don't know the answer. But when I arrived home from my Easter in Holland, I found that Prince Charles had said something to the point. He recently told a bunch of architects in America: 'If the money motive for development is the only serious force in urban renewal, then we shall not succeed. Building is about more than just money and market forces.'

The burghers who built Amsterdam and Delft didn't build them simply to make a quick buck; they built them to live in themselves. But when I look round modern London, I see street after street lying derelict – not because the buildings have outlived their usefulness, but because some company is going to make a killing by demolishing them *en masse* and then building the cheapest and biggest block it can to sell off as office space.

Real towns are like real ales. If you make them simply and solely to get rich and without any love for the things themselves, you end up making substitutes and destroy whatever it was you set out to make in the first place.

The blame for the ugliness and squalor of modern urban environments does not lie with the architects, but with our society that places no bounds on greed and that puts more value on the creation of profit than on the creation of beauty.

Prince Charles is right. And what's more, I know he must be right because Norman Tebbit, the Chairman of the Conservative Party, has told him to shut up, and Mr Tebbit never wastes his breath trying to silence people who are talking rubbish.

13 April 1988

Charles is warned by Tebbit

Tebbit attacks Charles for 'dangerous' political views

THE RULE OF LAW

The Rule of Law must be upheld. That's what the Prime Minister has said, and who would dare to gainsay her? Whatever the cost to the fabric of our society, the 'Rule of Law' is, as Mrs Thatcher says, 'inviolate'. Of course, we ought to be quite clear what she means by the 'Rule of Law'.

If, for example, some people jump out of a car, gun down three other people in the public streets and then jump back into the car and disappear, then that is the 'Rule of Law'. If ministers then tell the House of Commons tall stories about what happened – claiming there was a bomb, when there was no bomb, and that the three dead people were armed, when they were not armed – then that is the 'Rule of Law'. Furthermore, if ministers and their apologists state on TV that the three dead people were behaving suspiciously and looked as if they were about to draw weapons, then that too is the 'Rule of Law'.

On the other hand, if TV journalists ask people who were there at the time of the killings what they saw, and those people make statements that contradict the government's version of events – saying, for example, that the dead people had their hands in the air and were shot down in cold blood – then those journalists are acting against the 'Rule of Law'.

For let us be quite clear: the 'Rule of Law' means the

'Rule of Government' – and not just any government but *this* government.

If, for example, members of the secret service tried to destabilize the previous Labour administration, then that would not be against the 'Rule of Law'. It wouldn't even merit an inquiry. But if one of those involved tried to publish a book which mentioned this plot, then that *would* be against the 'Rule of Law', because it might make the present government appear to be the beneficiary of MI5's dirty work, and that wouldn't be good for the government's image.

In such a case, the 'Rule of Law' decrees that the taxpayers' money should be thrown around the courtrooms of the world in vain attempts to silence those who spy and tell. The 'Rule of Law' would even require an otherwise respected civil servant to be dispatched to a courtroom in the antipodes to lie on behalf of the government.

For the 'Rule of Law' means that truth and deceit are no longer different things. Truth is only right and proper when it serves the interests of the government. Whenever the truth is damaging to the government, the 'Rule of Law' requires that it should be rigorously suppressed. What is more, those who seek to tell such truths need to be discredited. Lies and disinformation about them should be allowed to circulate through the gutters of Wapping as quickly as possible.

The 'Rule of Law' enshrines the government's right to economize with the truth as much as it likes. The 'Rule of Law' also safeguards the government's increasing right to stop anyone else – particularly journalists and broadcasters – from being more generous with the truth. This is because the 'Rule of Law' has nothing to do with truth or even justice. It is only concerned with the national interest. And the national interest, as the government tried to establish at Clive Ponting's trial, is identical to the government's interest. Thus, under Mrs Thatcher's 'Rule of Law' any-one who speaks or acts against the interests of the government is naturally doing so against the nation as a whole.

So, before the Thought Police come and batter down my door, I'm going to stop writing these treasonable columns, and spend the rest of the year making a nice harmless film about Vikings.

I'd just like to say goodbye and good luck – I think we're all going to need it.

13 May 1988